P9-DMR-538

METHODS

METHODS

Approaches for the Catechesis of Adolescents

PIERRE BABIN

Translated and Adapted by
John F. Murphy

HERDER AND HERDER

1967
HERDER AND HERDER NEW YORK
232 Madison Avenue, New York 10016

Original edition: *Méthodologie,*
Lyons, Editions du Chalet, 1966.

Nihil obstat: Leo J. Steady, Censor Librorum
Imprimatur: ✠Robert F. Joyce, Bishop of Burlington
September 1, 1967

Library of Congress Catalog Card Number: 67-25875

Manufactured in the United States of America

CONTENTS

APPENDIX: HOW TO BUILD A CATECHETICAL LIBRARY

PREFACE

As we face ourselves more and more critically in the Church today, we are aware that the traditional forms of religious education, formerly supported and strengthened by authority-centered cultures, are no longer truly effective.

The world in which the parish, the school, and the community were one in mind and heart is rapidly changing and Christians are finding themselves in a society where a man must think and act on the basis of his own convictions, rather than on the convictions and traditions of the community.

Our religious education programs are being challenged by students and teachers alike: the students do not find meaning in much of what we are saying; the teachers are finding a growing apathy or questioning which is disturbing.

Our truths have not changed; our methods, unfortunately, have not. Man learns according to his time. Our time is a new one. Our approach to the eternal truth must be seen in terms of our age's insights and needs and capabilities. If we are not a tradition and authority-centered society, must we find truth in a traditional and authoritarian manner? Or is it possible that we can find truth through a communal search, a fraternal undertaking? Can the Holy Spirit work through man as he is?

Father Pierre Babin holds that we not only can find truth through a communal and fraternal search, but that we must since that is man's approach today, and it will be through that approach that the Holy Spirit will work. It is the incarnational method, God working with His people as He finds them in order to be one with them, forming them anew as He has done with each age, with each unique generation's search for truth.

In this volume Father Babin offers some insights on methods and techniques that can meet the needs and interests of the contemporary adolescent. These ideas, rather than solving a teacher's problems, call for exploration on the part of any individual who wants to share Christ with his students. Some of the suggestions, to the more experienced teachers, may seem rather obvious. Yet Father Babin goes beyond the seemingly obvious; he goes beyond the immediate and asks us to look at the underlying meaning of these methods. He wants us not only to use new techniques, but to know and understand their meaning.

In all of his works, he has urged us to take our students beyond the surface. He does this for teachers in the present work.

I have taken the liberty of adapting material where it was necessary for the American scene, especially in terms of the Confraternity of Christian Doctrine or in areas of concern peculiar to the American school system. In addition, I have incorporated some relevant material from an article of mine which appeared in *The Living Light*[1] that develops some of Father Babin's approaches in terms of the American experience.

A book on methods runs a great risk. It is somewhat similar to a cook book. Every cook has a favorite recipe, or long-estab-

[1] John F. Murphy, "A Guide for Catechists on Purposes, Material, Lesson-Planning, and Techniques," *The Living Light,* vol. 3, no. 3, Autumn, 1966, pp. 44-55.

lished traditions in terms of preparation and handling of materials. Yet a good cook knows that no one book contains every possible recipe. Neither does a good book on methods contain every possible method. What Father Babin has done is to provide us with a basic introduction, an approach, in the hope that we may profit and grow. What we need, perhaps more than anything else, is not a book that offers every possible answer, but one that opens many solid and valid avenues for exploration and experimentation. This has been his aim.

St. Pius X Preparatory School
Uniondale, New York

(REV.) JOHN F. MURPHY

METHODS

INTRODUCTION

How does today's teacher effectively transmit and share his faith, a faith that must be rooted in the Gospel, with adolescents caught up in the twentieth century? What does he do? How does he go about it?

We live in a time when man in his capacity for decisive action most frequently sought to teach Christ in terms of human intuition and direct experience. Today, He wishes to be spoken of in creasingly rational and scientific dimension in man's evolution. Further, mankind is experiencing, as never before, the delight of power. "Nothing is impossible to God," said the angel at the Annunciation. Today's youth, seized by the fantastic success of science and technology, will say, "Nothing is impossible for man."

Have we overstated the situation? Perhaps. Yet the facts are before us from the carefully rationalized organization of industry to the scientific conquest of the cosmos. A new type of man is being born, born into a world where these new values become laws, and where science is seen as a tool at man's disposal. But why cannot this moment of man's ascending power be also a great moment of the power of Christ? Why cannot these days be the setting of one of the great moments of His presence in history?

Up to the present day, in our religious education we have

most frequently sought to teach Christ in terms of human intuition and direct experience. Today, He wishes to be spoken of in new terms and new forms, those of this modern rational man, the man of technology; and it depends upon us, and it will be through us, that He will incarnate Himself in twentieth-century thought. It will be through us that Christ will acquire and make His own this new development in man, that He will in some way become part of the organizational structures, the collective man, the rationalized methods and procedures of today; and He will not, as before, simply be seen through the efforts of the individual genius or through the empirical and on-the-spot skills of the teacher, or through the traditional methods of another age.

Obviously then, what we must have if we are to adapt successfully to today's world are precise and effective methods and ease in the use of valid techniques. We do not mean a technology or a rationalization which dehumanizes and kills the spirit; rather, we mean those techniques and that use of the rational in man which develops him; and we mean also the increase of the power of the Holy Spirit. This is the challenge for our faith: Is the Church to lag behind the world in the use of God's gifts to man, and does she still have the mission of incarnating the Word of God in man as man is? In the proclamation of Christ's Message is she going to continue at the pace of yesterday's man, or is she going to use the new accelerated pace given to us through the development of new techniques of thought and action?

Is this simply a concern only for adaptation and updating in our religious education? Is it simply a desire for a more methodical and organized, and hence more effective catechesis? These are loudable insofar as they are formulated with the point of view of rendering our catechesis a truly effective instrument in the Christian growth of our students and not merely an efficient technique. But the true motivation for taking a modern approach is more profound: the desire for a more methodical religious education springs from faithfulness to the Incarnation itself, from the desire to make oneself completely dependent upon the Risen Christ who wishes to penetrate every mode and form of the world's existence and to touch each age of man in its uniqueness.

Method and technique, in the modern sense of these words,[1] are absolutely indispensable if religious education is going to be faithful to the Spirit of Christ, if catechetics is going to prolong the Word made flesh in our age. To refuse the effort, or to underestimate the value of method and technique, is to refuse that "fundamental method" which is God's redemptive Incarnation. It was in the plan of God that He would redeem man by becoming one with and using what was in man.

The studies and reflections which you are about to read do not have as their aim a universal panacea based on infallible formulas. To seek success by way of devising mere procedures betrays a real misunderstanding of method or technique. Technique is ultimately at the service of the creative and creating teacher and is not a replacement for thought. What you will

[1] According to the scholastics, technique belongs to the category of art and is defined as a "totality of procedures serving to produce a certain result." In the modern sense it is a "rationalized art" (Siegfried). It is characterized by the rationalization of procedures to attain a goal: "organized methods which rest on a corresponding scientific knowledge."

find here are not formulas, but ideas for concrete actions, suggestions for the teaching situation. In short, what you will find are general norms which will permit any one teacher to discover what is, for him, the best method of being faithful to the Spirit and to the youth of today.

The first part of this book aims at setting forth rather briefly the general spirit, character, and common traits which underlie all the techniques and methods proper to the religious education of adolescents. Insofar as one can speak of a method rooted in the Gospel, that is, in the style of Christ, one can speak of a style, the general approach or inspiration, which strikes us as characterizing a religious education for today's adolescents. Method, therefore, in the first section of the book is taken in a rather large and abstract sense, not primarily as a series of procedures but more as a direction which is definable and regularly followed.[2] The first section is not just an introduction but rather it defines and sets up what will follow.

The second part of the book deals with the actual class situation. How do you prepare for it? How do you organize your material and give life to it? Here the word "method" takes on a more concrete and practical meaning: the carefully worked out approach, the rationally organized plans, the present and practical means to be used in view of the aim to be reached.

The third area in this study will present some methods and techniques (but not all) which can be used by the teacher, subject to adaptation by each individual. Method in this part is taken in the more precise sense of the collection of procedures destined to insure, in an economical way, a pre-determined result.

[2] *Methods* presupposes the reading of *Options* (New York, 1967).

Yet preliminary to any use of methods there must be reflection, a deep-felt need on the part of the teacher for truth itself. Thus techniques are never imposed absolutely. Teachers are methodical, but they are above all true to themselves as men of their times. A teacher who brings Christ's Message should be a person of method, because he should listen to the Holy Spirit and merge and involve himself completely with His designs.

One could say of this book that it is a gamble. Everything depends on the spirit in which it is read, as with the words inscribed on the Palais de Chaillot:

That I be a tomb or treasure,
That I speak or hold my tongue,
Depends on the one who passes by.
My friend, do not enter here without desire.

(Paul Valéry)

It could be better said: Do not enter here without spirit, without the Spirit.

PART ONE

THE COVENANT METHOD

I.

THE COVENANT METHOD

WHAT, then, is this common road (method: from *meta odos,* way towards), this general direction or perhaps even this common style, which will characterize all the organizational forms, all the techniques and procedures for the religious education of adolescents? We propose to call it the Covenant Method. It is something we must first define and defend. Then, in a few simple propositions, we will set out its principles and characteristics.

1. GOD'S PLAN FOR HIS PEOPLE

The term "Covenant Method" has been chosen deliberately. It is a necessity that our religion teaching be seen in its full human, scientific, and rational dimensions—a view possible only in terms of the very history of salvation. Each teacher of religion, it is hoped, should be able to enter carefully and thoughtfully into the very method used by God Himself. In doing so he will then be able to correct and perfect himself not only in terms of reason alone, but also in terms of the faith.

Our aim here is not only to define a method of the covenant

by appealing to reason, but to go further in looking to the light of historical revelation.

In turning to the Scriptures, the teacher can discover the Covenant Method used by the God of Jesus Christ with His people and then see more clearly how he himself can enter into covenant with his students, how he can learn to establish a meaningful relationship of faith for and with his students. The meaning of the covenant developed gradually in the world of the Israelites, becoming ever more purified and subtle; it reached a new dimension with Christ and His relationship with the Apostles and the Church. The teacher can and must learn how his own relationship, his own covenant, with the students can develop and form as the students mature or reach new levels of insight and capability. Taking the idea of covenant in the history of salvation, let us examine the following characteristics of this method with a view to understanding our own approaches to students, our own covenant method for today.

(1) A covenant is an alliance, an agreement, *with a group*—a well-defined historical and socio-cultural reality. Even though a covenant or agreement is usually made through one individual, yet this individual is a representative of the whole group. Yahweh, in the accounts of Covenant in the Bible, commits Himself to a collective reality through one or more individuals, but it is not an agreement directed to the private life of one individual, but to and for the whole group which he represents.

(2) If we may say so, the Covenant makes God exist, not above His people, but *with His people,* marching with them, sharing a destiny. God even takes the name Emmanuel, *God with us.*

(3) The Covenant, while making possible a relationship of

dialogue and friendship and also bringing into play the whole process of personal interaction, still does not take away the element of *initiative* and of *creation which belongs to God*. Without doubt, in the Covenant the divine partner of the agreement "empties Himself" of His glory, working quietly and discreetly so as not to overwhelm or constrain human freedom. Without doubt, His omipotence will show itself in weakness and poverty so that the bonds established will indeed be those of love. Nevertheless, it still remains that God is the initiator in this relationship; it is He who creates in the other, man, the possibilities of *becoming,* and who *strengthens* and *confirms* man by His presence and His saving work.

(4) Finally, the Covenant is directed to man receiving the *gift of the Spirit*. The summit and end of the Covenant is to make man exist in autonomy, in full responsibility, and in full liberty, according to the Spirit. It is in the Spirit that man achieves his fullness as a person. The teacher, faithful to and learning from God's approach to man, will allow the adolescent to rise up to a state of self-responsibility. Through techniques which demand research, dialogue, sharing, and giving from his students, the teacher will enable them to realize their capacities for creation and their need for human relationships. Such a method could be called that of friendship, and hence we use the term "covenant." It is from our understanding of covenant that we see that the Covenant Method can be expressed in terms of friendship. In fact, the Covenant Method entails a certain equality in the relationship, a definite possibility for the adolescent for personal discovery, for reaction, and for freedom. (This was the unusual gift of God's Covenant with man.)

2. THE ADOLESCENT TODAY

The adolescent situation today and the position of the Jewish people marching towards the promised land with Yahweh are not too dissimilar. There is the same need of a loving presence, a presence which was lived in the midst of the Jewish people, which was incarnated in their midst; there is the same yearning for a land of freedom and autonomy. There are many areas in the story of the Jews which correspond to the psychology and the socio-cultural situation of the adolescent today.

1. *The Psychology of the Adolescent*

A. HUMAN RELATIONSHIPS

The role of the teacher and the forms or techniques of giving Christ's Message are intimately connected with the different characteristics of each stage of human development. Man, in fact, is not a closed universe with neither door nor windows. He is an open being, a being of relation. When we speak of human development, we speak of the development in relationships. Man cannot exist without essential relations with other people, with the world, with God. This openness to others, this fundamental and elemental part of his nature, expresses itself in different situations according to the different ages or stages of development: the situations of son, of father, of friend.[1]

[1] Cf. *Friendship* (New York, 1967). These categories do not here express juridical or sociological situations, but modes of being constitutive of the person in his relationships with the other. These categories, however, are not mutually

1. The Child. In the child, it is the *filial relationship* which dominates: the child listens and receives. Consequently, in giving the Message of Christ to the child, the teacher is above all the father who calms, secures, enlightens the intelligence, educates to attention, creates habit. He teaches as a master; it is he who chooses and imposes the form and determines the progress of the group.

2. The Adult. For adults, it is the *paternal relationship* which dominates: man now gives life; but, at the same time, he is shaped by his sons. A mature adult is one whose interest and receptivity are conditioned essentially by what he has to give or transmit to others. Consequently, in religious teaching which is addressed to the adult, the teacher is the one who promotes the synthetic view of problems, who clarifies the individual's actions and thinking by objective teaching. The teacher of adults is the one who helps the adult make personal decisions in order ultimately to enable the adult to give or to transmit to others what he himself has received.

3. The Adolescent. At this stage, the *friendship relationship* dominates: the youth gives and exchanges as he becomes aware of himself and then becomes what he is. (Adolescence is the time of self-identity.) In the religious education of adolescents, the teacher in some way must enter into the ways that characterize the friendship relationship: he will arouse, call forth, dialogue, strengthen.

---

exclusive and are often found to be overlapping. Is this not also true in the method of the covenant? One of the proofs of this is in the biblical images (father, friend, husband) which describe it; but the insistence on a particular image will be made in relation to a particular age.

B. THE TEACHER-ADOLESCENT RELATIONSHIP

The Covenant Method consists essentially in being with the adolescents and in making them become (that is, to realize what and who they are, to grow).

1. To Be With. The adolescent is one who has a need to live and to assert himself; this involves struggle and tension. He has a need to be understood and listened to for himself, to have someone with him to bolster him in his search for himself. He knows very well the country, the life of childhood, which he has come from; but he does not know the one towards which he is going. Like Israel, he marches across the desert towards his "promised land." His confusion comes from the fact that he does not know exactly what this promised land is. He sees it in a confused manner. What does he need in this search? Not a teacher who imposes from the outside, but a fraternal guide, a brotherly educator, who marches along with him and holds him up. The teacher of adolescents must "be with" them. The God of the Covenant guided Israel in its march towards the promised land and "was with" her: "Do not fear, little flock, for I am with you always."

What this method demands is an understanding and acceptance of the meaning of the friend relationship and its place in the development of the adolescent. It is not an abdication of authority to the adolescent, but the more difficult relationship of a friend and teacher who shares and yet guides, who respects and is respected. It calls forth and demands a growing awareness of the meaning of community, with its necessary structures, for the adolescent; it means a growing acceptance of the adolescent's own responsibility towards himself and others and the rules of the group.

This attitude of brother and guide is necessary if the adolescent is to learn who he is and not only to be told who he is. In the setting of the formal class, with thirty or forty students present, this covenant approach expresses itself in the attitude of the teacher towards the group and the individual, and in the time and personal involvement of a teacher with his group and individuals within the group. It becomes more clearly expressed in the teacher's use of certain techniques and methods which enable the students to grow in responsibility and initiative.

2. *To Make Them Become.* In the difficult search for who they are, adolescents seek to realize themselves, to expand all the forces and powers of life which they feel to be awakening in themselves. What do they expect from this fraternal teacher who is with them, if not that this adult will help them become themselves in freedom, that this teacher will help them grow in love and that he will strengthen them in their potentialities, their capacities for living and loving and being free and responsible? Adolescents expect not a teacher who constrains, but one who opens and strengthens, who helps them find the "promised land" of their personal vocations. It is similar to what happened as the God of the Covenant led His people into the promised land, strengthening them in their vocation of an elect people, preparing them to welcome the Word and the Spirit. It is similar to Christ watching over the group of the Twelve, confirming them in their election and helping them become in the power of the Spirit: "You did not choose me, I chose you; and I commissioned

you to go out and to bear fruit, fruit that will last." In sharing in the method of the Covenant, we are asked to help our students become what Christ has offered them, a share in His work; and we are given His approach.

2. *The Socio-Cultural Situation of the Adolescent*

If a new approach to the teaching of religion seems to be required here, it is also because the adolescent period has entered into a new socio-cultural setting. The Covenant Method is justified by the changes which have come into the society in which adolescents live.[2]

In yesterday's strongly hierarchical society, the behavior of youth was based essentially on reference to authority, to very definite norms. The ideal teacher then was the master who proposed a definite structure, the father-image who transmitted tradition and imposed a way of behavior. Present society is quite different; it is pluralist, liberal, and democratic. It is no longer a society of carefully defined structures wherein an adolescent would know and could be taught forms of behavior that would carry on to the adult world. In our society, adolescents must continually discover forms of behavior, adapt them, and readjust them to ever fluid situations. Also, they are asking their own questions today, choosing their own associates, and creating their own groups.

In such a context, how can the teacher still continue to use an educational approach which is mainly paternal? He is, now, in some way called to enter into a teaching role which is pri-

[2] Cf. *Options,* "The Group Approach," p. 130.

marily that of friend, confronted as he is with this new socio-cultural context of youth.

The Church herself, faced at Vatican II with the rapid and profound changes in today's world, rethought her pastoral theology, her own presence in the world; she recognized the growth of freedom and cultural pluralism. She did not impose herself, but she called out to the world. Has not the Church entered more decisively now upon the way of dialogue with the world? Following her example, and for the same socio-cultural reasons, the teacher who wants to educate the adolescent today is called upon to take the paths that lead to freedom in the faith, to dialogue with youth, to active searching.

3. BASIC ELEMENTS OF THE COVENANT METHOD

This Covenant Method so far set forth asks for a certain number of attitudes and also makes a certain number of demands which will be constantly underlying and forming the foundation of the catechetical situation. These demands and attitudes are the core of this approach: to strengthen and confirm; to search and question; to work with the group; to exist in the present situation.

1. *To Confirm, to Strengthen*

The word "confirm" is borrowed in its present meaning from Martin Buber and has been used by Carl Rogers to designate what is needed for a helpful relation, a positive and free relation in which values are opened between human beings, and in which growth is hoped for. Essentially, the teacher will have to employ methods and have an attitude that confirms or strengthens the adolescent's potential. To confirm the other means to strengthen the other, to see his value, his worth, his ability to love, and thus to help this person become; it is to call a person to bring forth what he has within himself. It is to call forth rather than to impose on or to pass judgment. To do this the teacher needs method, needs to create the climate, to use any and every facility so that the capacities of his students will be brought to life.[3]

In actual situations, this desire to confirm or strengthen the other must meet the following requirements:

(1) The methods used, the carefully considered and thought-out lessons, must be based on the *real needs and actual capacities of the adolescents.* This is no place for a teacher to create an artificial atmosphere of complete freedom for his students in order to let them realize their potential; that is a misunderstanding of the place of freedom in an individual who is in the process of assuming freedom. Yet to confirm another means also to avoid using methods which ignore the students' capabilities for some degree of freedom.

This approach requires delicate balance. As teachers we are not meant to create anguish with a complete *laissez-faire* attitude which can give rise to despair in some students who are not yet capable of handling all situations; or it can give a false sense of freedom in which an adolescent can assume too much for himself. Again we must be realistic and not make excessive

[3] Carl Rogers, *The Personnel and Guidance Journal,* p. 616.

demands on our group by an over-use of group techniques which demand a certain maturity.

(2) The methods used in this approach will have to be adapted to *a sound and always developing understanding of this particular group* of students we are working with. This class, this group in this situation, is a living and moving reality made up at each moment of the reactions of each individual in the group, with their likes and dislikes, their potentialities and weaknesses. Hence it is important to understand the state and thinking of the entire group, not only each individual's psychological state, but even more the psychological interplay within the group. As most teachers are aware, each class has its own personality; and, although it is not always easy to accept a particular group, yet it is the class here and now that must be understood—and never in terms of some previous well-liked group to which we compare it. When we categorize and judge by certain pre-set standards, we are missing the person or persons in front of us.

(3) All of our techniques and plans will aim at maintaining a constant atmosphere of *dialogue and openness* between the teacher and the students. To be open and aware of the other does not necessarily mean that the teacher and students must be always speaking or explaining ideas to one another, but more that there be a communion, a rapport, between them. This supposes that the teacher is proceeding along with his students, participating in their discoveries, and that he himself is being transformed with them. A teacher should learn anew each time he brings human beings along the path of truth.

(4) Our methods and approaches should permit our students

to become aware of themselves and to express themselves. Thus the teacher will propose activities to them in which they can measure themselves and realize their own worth in front of others and to themselves. It will be in these activities that they confirm or strengthen themselves.

(5) Finally, there are needed some methods which will allow them to grow little by little in *self-responsibility for their own religious education* which will let them take a greater initiative, a greater responsibility in the education of their faith. Thus the use of attitudes and procedures directed to a certain autonomy will make them workers and leaders at the same time.

To confirm, then, is to help them realize what is within themselves. Yet to confirm or strengthen means that we must guide and help rather than merely loosen our control. To misform a sense of freedom is as dangerous as to permit no free formation at all.

2. *To Search, to Question*

This is a method which aims at making the adolescent react to the call of Christ. Rather than imposing a prefabricated, ready-made scheme of questions with answers, the teacher will proceed by means of contrasting points of view, by way of affirming or questioning them. This is not a catechesis all sewn up and ready for delivery. At the time of adolescence when personality and intellectual freedom are developing, the entry into the truth must involve personal reaction and must be worked out in struggle and combat.

Consequently:

(1) A meeting with the adolescents will be planned, based on the following general scheme:

—*Establish a bond* with the class.

—*Disturb* them and bring them to *think* by asking essential questions, by helping them discover the depths and the limits of the experiences and needs of man.

—*Announce the Gospel Message* in terms of the questions of mankind; make known the richness and superabundance of the Good News.

—*Explain*. Have the students discover the presence of God's revelation in human life and action today.

(2) In order to stimulate intellectual reaction, the teacher will use a certain variety of approaches, such as group methods, more traditional classroom dialogue, and so forth.

3. *To Work With the Group*

The methods and attitudes will aim at educating individuals who are related to one another, who are seen in the group relationship.[4] The covenant is a covenant with the group.

Consequently:

(1) A very special importance will be given to group techniques and to creating attitudes which develop freedom and charity in the group (see Part Three).

(2) Special importance will also be given to methods of forming leaders of the group, leaders eventually capable of sharing or supplanting the teacher's role as animator of the class (see *Options* and Part Three of this work).

[4] Cf. *Options, ibid.*

(3) Thus our methods and attitudes must be marked by respect for persons, cordiality in relationships, dialogue, and the democratic spirit (see Parts One and Two).

4. *To Exist in the Present Situation*

In an age when science and mass media impress on our students a new sensitivity to human experience and the world around them, our methods and procedures in religious education must take on a character that is living and concrete.

Consequently:

(1) An important place in our religious instruction should be given to *concrete activities* that will help our students make the jump from their own immediate and limited situations to a broader view and to help them personally to understand the meaning of Revelation. Our teaching must always be rooted in the beginning in the concrete situation if it is to serve.

(2) A special place should be given in religious education to the *contemporary world,* to contemporary events (see Part Two). If we are to situate our teaching in the adolescents' world, it will be because we are willing to use the world they know as the tool with which they can go further.

It is necessary, in conclusion, to underline the fact that the Covenant Method is essential for all teachers of adolescents. Presence to all, youthfulness of heart, simplicity and faith in man, infinite capacity for listening and sympathizing, always looking at the emerging man—all of this the adolescent needs, more than at any other age; and this method expects and demands all.

PART TWO

MEETING WITH THE STUDENTS

II.

HOW TO PREPARE OUR CLASSES

BEFORE announcing His message, Christ first began by incarnating Himself: He inserted Himself in a human group and assumed its language and hopes, and He understood what gave life to that group. He caught Himself up in men's thinking and tensions; He was "in all things like to a man, excepting sin."

The teacher also, before any immediate and technical preparation of the lesson to be given, must root himself in the reality of the class he will face.

We must then distinguish two steps in the preparation of the teacher:

—*the remote preparation,* which consists in establishing communion with the class;

—*the immediate preparation,* which consists in the technical construction and preparation for the actual class situation.

1. REMOTE PREPARATION

How to Achieve Rapport or Establish Communion With the Class

It is by the Incarnation that God has forged the most profound bonds with man, realizing with man a communion of destiny and language. In order to understand and to achieve this communion with our students, we will have to go to the school of God.

1. *A Common Bond of Destiny*

To have a true encounter, a real meeting, with another presents a problem to any human being; and the teacher is not exempt from this difficulty. The teacher must be capable of going beyond the external behavior, the words, the expressed opinions of the adolescents. He must grasp the inner person of the student, the person avid for fulfillment who dreams of success and yet is so liable to discouragement. A teacher, or anybody involved in human relations, cannot achieve this effort of incarnation without letting himself be invaded by the other in a certain manner; without, in some way, becoming the other in order to join the other in truth. A human being must communicate in that which is at the heart of the other's being, in that which constitutes the other as a unique person. This all supposes a greatness and an availability of spirit which never amounts just to complicity; it needs a tenderness which will always be healthy, worthy of the love of God.

This bond of union comes to life through an essential solidarity in suffering, hope, and the existence of life itself. The teacher must feel himself embarking with the adolescents upon the same voyage, in the same direction, and with the same insecurity.

Woe to the pharisaical teacher who is righteous in his own authority and who will no longer be a poor man among men.

To be able to communicate with the class in a Christian school is to be alive to those students in all aspects of their school life, to be with them, when possible, around the building. If it is a parish high school, it is to know them also in the parish, in their neighborhoods, in their free-time interests. To teach in a CCD structure does not remove this obligation; it intensifies it since the students are seen less frequently, and most probably have greater need for contact. It is in knowing another that we are capable of sharing and receiving. The willingness to be available, to be personable, to search out at times, is one of the gifts of the Confraternity teacher or school instructor which is most precious and necessary.

In the same area, how can the teacher make a vital presence to the adolescents if he continues to live out of touch with the world in a kind of ivory tower, self-contained and isolated, surrounded with his own sense of security and never risking the weakness of existence? There are some teachers who do not seem capable of being touched or overwhelmed by the happenings of the world around them. Yet in order to live the incarnation, to communicate with the other, it is necessary to experience with him the same sentiments of joy and sadness, to share in the same interior struggles, the same enthusiasms, the same objects of pride, the same anguish. The question may be asked: Cannot an individual achieve a sense of security with himself and his faith? Yes, but it must be also a faith that grows and renews and searches with the growth and renewal of the world and the

Church. Faith is not a static gift; it includes the gift of oneself with one's tensions and struggles. We do not participate in our students' tensions in order to bestow extraordinary importance upon them, but to develop in our students a faith which prepares them to live with the difficulties of each day.

And even though we as teachers may not be touched in the same manner as the adolescents by their problems of existence, nor stirred up by the great currents which today shape the collective mentality, what must clearly appear is that we are living some type of drama in our own existence. For the love of God we must be continuously willing to accept a threatened existence. Our students must sense this openness in us.

The teacher has to share in the world of the poor men who need to be saved, and not belong to the virtuous world which will definitively rule on all the problems of the adolescent. Let the teacher show himself also as one on the road of love and grace which does not offer easy solutions but which calls a man to go always beyond the last point reached. Finally, the teacher must have the desire to see that the adolescents succeed in their existence, in their profound hopes and aspirations. If the teacher does not do these things, then the adolescents will not see in him one who shares in a common destiny.

2. *A Comon Bond of Language*

The common bond of destiny becomes alive with adolescents through language. Language is a test of communion; it reveals that which each person carries within himself of the realities of earth, of the problems of man, of the future of the world.

Even further, language signifies a history. Each man, in fact, expresses and reveals himself in his language, by the words and gestures which are rich in personal meaning and signification. Language is one of the signs which tells others about ourselves, our home, our background and culture. Our words are colored by our cultural, professional, social, economic, and political differences; and our words affect other people according to their own backgrounds. It is an illusion to believe that an individual says exactly the same thing to everyone when he addresses the same words to them.

The gestures, the looks, the slang expressions, the "in" language of the students are sometimes difficult to understand. Yet this language is real, more real and more expressive than a lengthy or carefully delineated speech.

"The more you come to know your students, to know their language, to appeal to their experience and to make use of that experience yourself in order to help them understand new ideas, the more you will be assured of success." Such is the method which Douglas Hyde proposed to militant communists. One could not adopt a more educational approach.

Language is an encounter, a meeting. The teacher cannot remain deaf to the language of men of today. If he does, he will never touch them with his own words. He cannot be truly present to the adolescents if he ignores the sights and sounds that are connected to their intense experiences of life, love, work, leisure, and so on. In order to encounter another in truth, one must begin by learning the language of the other.

Thus sharing the Word of God with the present generation calls for inventive effort on the teacher's part. He will have to reject the temptation to stress only the objective level of the Word of God, and he will have to force himself to penetrate into the meaning that gives life here and now, in language that makes the Word of God a contemporary and vital thing. Without this effort to understand and use human language, the teacher cannot pretend to reach the vital center of man's existence.

This approach to adolescents through language, however, will be clearly insufficient without the force of the teacher's own life of witness which itself confirms that which his words announce.

3. *How to Learn This Language*

The teacher can acquire this knowledge of the adolescents' language by listening to his students, reading what they read, seeing the same films and television programs, knowing the current songs. Thus he will be able, when the moment comes, to express the Kingdom of God through the idiom of his students.

But we have to go further. This effort of understanding youth will not be sufficient without a renewed understanding of doctrine. Karl Rahner has observed: "Does the Message of Christianity include any prophecy of our age, enabling us to say something theologically about our age as such? Or are we as Christians able only to declare what is always and universally valid, and them apply it to the case in hand?—in which process we shall always be dogged by the feeling that our principles are assuredly sound and good, but the attempt to apply them can be successful only to a limited extent, with the most important point of all left open: it could never yield any unambiguous conclusions because, having regard to this age as a whole, any such application of principles would rest upon an interpretation and analysis of our situation itself made not by theological but by purely personal means, thus always remaining our own, highly questionable work."[1]

Frankly, however, what good is an understanding of the adolescents' world, of their mode of seeing and judging, of their individual or collective interests, if the teacher has not yet fully assimilated the doctrine which he wants to share with them. Method presumes something to be shared, and something which we are ready to share. It is also necessary, we must add, to breathe new life today into Christian thought so that we can then have a new and enriched language attuned to today's man.

2. IMMEDIATE PREPARATION

There are three levels to be considered:

—the Message to be transmitted,
—the atmosphere to be created,
—the work of the teacher himself.

1. *The Message to be Transmitted*

A. THE TOTAL PLAN OF THE COURSE

(1) The teacher of religious education needs a plan; he must *know where he is going*. This is indispensable for the teacher, but it is also essential for the class. Adolescents, especially those in the upper years, want to know the general direction of the

[1] Karl Rahner, S.J., *The Christian Commitment* (New York, 1963), p. 6

course and the connection between the topics that are being covered. As students mature, they show more and more an intellectual need for understanding their own growth which the teacher must respect.

(2) This plan should be seen more as a *process,* as a *gradual entrance* of the students into the mystery of man and God. But it should not be worked out as a systematic exploration of the data of Revelation conducted on the abstract level. Adolescence, the age of exploration and conversion more than of synthesis, needs a message that reaches the needs of adolescents themselves.

As an example, here are two lesson approaches on the Church:

The Mystery of the Church:

—the foundation of the Church

—the profound nature of the Church

—the characteristics of the Church

—the life of the Church in the world.

The Mission of the Church:

—evangelization

—sanctification

—government.

Taking a different view, a teacher might propose the same topic to a group of girls in this fashion:

—What does the average person think of the Church? Contrast that with what God thinks of it. What, then, is the Church?

—What is the role of women in the Church? How does a woman live the great functions of priest, prophet, and king?

—What is the relation of the laity to the hierarchical ministry?

—What is the mission given by the Church to men and women in the world?

—What of those who do not seem to belong to the Church?

—What of a Church which needs to give life to its own image?

In the first plan the topic was explored systematically, according to an abstract order. The second plan takes the student progressively into the mystery of the Church; it starts by looking at what men think, then at what adolescents think, at what the student must do, and finally it arrives at the Council teachings about the Church.

(3) This over-all plan will have to be *pliable,* it must remain *supple,* because it supposes a continuing dialogue with the interests and questions of the student. It is necessary, of course, to show them the direction and the steps to be followed, and the teacher does not have to have his plan subordinate to the whims of the group. Yet he must remember that adolescents will never understand the Message if they are not open to it.

(4) *Discussion among teachers working on the same level* is invaluable, in either the regular school system or the Confraternity program. A plan that is meaningful and valid will require several sessions of discussion at the beginning of the year. Yet that is not sufficient. Meetings, characterized by honest evaluation, are needed if the teacher is to grow with his own class. The sharing of success and disappointment between teachers can produce a continually viable plan.

In conclusion:

(1) Starting off with the general needs of the students, give a general plan at the beginning of the year or the semester which indicates the over-all view.

(2) Do not hesitate to interrupt the plan in order to treat of a subject which, because of particular circumstances, seems to

interest everyone—for example, the significance of such and such a popular movie, or a special political event. Yet, if the teacher finds his students moving away from the general plan, he must sit down and rethink his plan, and perhaps consult with other teachers. He must find what is at fault in his plan, or perhaps even restructure it around this particular group's needs. Willingness to digress from the plan theme is laudable in itself, but such digression demands careful consideration and skill. Rigidity can be dangerous and harmful, yet continued digression from the plan can be detrimental to students and teachers alike.

(3) Never begin a topic without first providing motivation that enables the students to see the value of this area of discussion for their lives; for example: What does the Mass mean to you and your friends in the neighborhood?

(4) In a semester or a year's program, consider the major areas of difficulty for yourself and the students. Intersperse those times with periods of general background, some necessary religious culture, free exchanges or discussions on current problems.

B. SPECIFIC GUIDES FOR OUTLINING AND SCHEDULING THE OVER-ALL PLAN

As a general guide, the following outlines may be of some assistance, especially for teachers in the Confraternity programs.[2]

(1) Set definite goals, with some idea of how much can be realistically covered and meaningfully explored.

(2) Determine how your purpose can be carried out most effectively in your particular and unique situation, in terms of hours, classes, background of students, and curriculum.

[2] Cf. Murphy, *art. cit.*, p. 45.

(3) See the over-all plan in terms of actual classroom time. Some lessons in manuals do not fit into fifty-minute sessions.

(4) Consider possible dates for retreats, parish affairs, examinations in the local schools, and so forth, which may cut down attendance in the Confraternity program.

(5) Block off your units in some type of plan book with specific dates, your examination times, and so forth.

(6) Work with other teachers in establishing unity, especially on the grade level. The team approach in a parish Confraternity and in the Catholic high school on each grade level will be of immense help in clarifying the goals of the teacher and the effectiveness in teaching. Teachers learn by sharing and exchanging background, methods, content. Group discussion on books dealing with catechetical aims and methods can help teachers deepen their own understanding of purpose.

(7) Evaluate as you go along in terms of your own goals, your techniques, students' reactions, students' involvement in the topic.

(8) If you can, make a summary of the material given to your class after you have finished each session. This process is time-consuming, but will provide a relatively objective record for this year and future ones.

C. BACKGROUND READING AND PREPARATION ON A PARTICULAR TOPIC

1. Preparation Time. A beginning teacher ought to count two or three hours of preparation for one hour of class time. To discover his own way of translating and teaching some point of Christ's message, the teacher must have profoundly assimilated it himself. This demands reflection, research, and time. It cannot be avoided. Each teacher knows from experience that there are days when he must deny himself some leisure in order to remain faithful to this task.

If time is markedly limited, as can happen, or if a teacher has two or even three separate preparations, then his outside reading and the development of original techniques should be limited to one class. With the other class or classes, the teacher can follow the manual or guides for the particular text. Preference will have to be the guide in this matter, and the extra study and reading should be made the center of one's spiritual life during that time.

Besides, instead of multiplying and possibly weakening preparations in different fields, the teacher will have the chance to develop one program completely during that year and another during the second.

2. Books to Consult. In order to deepen the mystery which he wants to transmit, the teacher will have to turn to doctrinal works. But which ones? In the long run, his work will be made simpler if he limits his choices to works in which the mystery is rethought and set down according to the thinking of our time, rather than reading manuals of theology. Examples of such new-style works are *The Resurrection* by F. X. Durrwell and *Theology of Revelation* by Gabriel Moran. Works on catechetics—its pedagogy, scope, aims—should also be consulted. At times, the Gospels will be the direct source for knowing what the thinking of Christ is on a subject—for example, on prayer.

The problem of doctrinal reading is not easily solved, however. Even works by well-known authors are not always easy to obtain, or there may be no or limited access to a library. While the teacher in a religious community may have less of a problem here, he does not always have the time to make use of the community library. The Confraternity teacher is frequently at more of a disadvantage. The growing number of teacher-training institutes is a partial remedy, and much remains for teacher training and placement. The fault does not always fall to the teacher struggling to learn, but lies in the lack of availability of material or courses for the teacher to turn to.

3. How to Read Doctrinal Works. If a teacher wants to profit from his reading, he will have to keep constantly in mind the thinking of his own students and he will have to search out those areas to which his students are especially sensitive and those which repel them (yet which may be useful later). A teacher has to read in two ways: for his own growth and for his students'. It is possible for a teacher to read extensively and yet not read well in terms of his class.

D. WRITING THE LESSON PLAN

Experience generally will show that it is better to write out the lesson, although this does not necessarily mean that it will be given exactly as it stands.

1. Why? The lesson plan, written out, forces the teacher to think out carefully and precisely what he wants to cover; it will make him work out his doctrinal points more carefully in terms of his own ability and the group's readiness to receive. Careful preparation produces a stronger and more fruitful meeting with students, even though we are tempted to rely on facile improvisations that are occasionally successful. The teacher who has written out his lesson will be in a much better position to form a bond with the adolescents since he will have thought out the link between the Message and his students; and this is essential to his work.

2. *Writing the Actual Plan.* There are many approaches to lesson-plan writing. Some manuals in Confraternity texts give explicit directions for each class meeting. In any and every case the teacher should consider the prepared lesson in terms of his own class and situation.

Some text books for the regular high school class also provide manuals for the teacher. The same caution applies here.

The written outline enables the teacher to sift out ideas, to reëxamine his own thinking to make some possible insights into where he wants the class to go. It provides a guide in an area where a guide is an absolute necessity in a limited time period: the exchange and growth of ideas.

One possible plan that might prove profitable to some is as follows:

The teacher can divide his plan book into two columns noting:

on the right: the lesson as he will give it, with explanations, possible references, documents, etc.;

on the left: a brief résumé of the lesson, with key phrases and ideas that can be given to the students for their notebooks if this is the teacher's procedure.

If the class is involved in group research, for example, perhaps the lesson plan will be mainly questions to guide the thinking of the class. If the discussion continues to another time, the résumé will include a summary of the discussion thus far. In preparing for a class, it is essential to keep in mind what has gone on before, and the preparation may have to include a summary or a review of matter previously covered.

Let us take for an example a plan for a class on the Eucharist at the junior or senior level.

General aim of this session. An understanding of the relationship of the Eucharist to the everyday actions of a Christian.

Point of departure. Use the following problem: I don't see the link between my everyday actions, everything that forms the basis of my life, and the Eucharist. Is there such a connection?

Examples for class dsicussion (to help the students answer the problem).

—During the day you multiply gestures of friendship—for example, shaking hands with a friend, exchanging ideas and news, sharing cigarettes. (At Mass, also, you communicate.)

—During the day you act with others; for example, your work brings you together with classmates; you recreate with others. (At Mass, you live with community.)

—During the day you experience the fact that work keeps you from being too facile, that work makes you see yourself as you are; you are forced also to go beyond yourself to give to others. (At Mass, you abandon yourself to Christ in order to be more for God and more at the disposition of your brothers.)

From this possible discussion, perhaps carried by the students or bolstered by the teacher's insights, the teacher will be able to work into the following questions:

—Do you see a link between your friendship with a classmate and the communion of the Mass?

Or better:

—Some students say, "The good Masses are those that come at the end of a retreat or class discussion or outing because we have lived together and then we're able to express ourselves at Mass, to speak our intentions." What do you think?

—What is the great thing that Christ accomplishes at Mass? Do you ever feel this during the course of the day?

A summary of the points to be covered should be included in the plan for this day or the points for the next class's discussion. If the class is not to meet for another week, then some summary should be prepared and included in the lesson notes.

3. Outlining Material in Lesson Plans. The following guide for preparing lesson plans may prove helpful to teachers who have not had sufficient teacher training.[3]

(1) Put down on paper the aim of the lesson, or the idea that you want to get across. (This sometimes happens only after you have read all the material on a topic and then you narrow it. Discussion with another teacher can help.)

(2) Next consider what aspects of that idea you want to cover; for example, in the sacrament of Baptism you have the following possible areas: cleansing, revivifying, incorporation, water, oil, character of Baptism, priesthood of the laity, ritual, obligations.

(3) Now list the possible areas that you will have to cover in order to arrive at your lesson or idea. Do the students have enough background to get to your point? Can you or do you have to fill in the background for them, for example, from the textbooks or your own notes?

(4) Put your lead question down on paper. Then think about

[3] *Ibid.*, pp. 48–49.

what you are looking for with a particular question. What are the possible answers? Are they answers that will require discussion? Are they dead-end questions and answers? Where will they lead you and the class? Is the class ready for this question?

(5) Put down in writing the sequence of ideas, not the topics, which you intend to follow. One point should lead to the next, but you should have the points prepared in advance so that they lead to your goal. (It is important to point out that some points may come up which you had not considered; evaluate them in terms of your goals and your ability to incorporate them. Good teaching, like good conversation, should not be too rigid; but it should be productive and not too diffuse.)

(6) In putting down your ideas, try to outline the ideas as a student might see the sequence. This is the most difficult part of the preparation and the one that requires the most flexibility in operation since not all minds see the same relationships and sequences. A definite aim is essential, and possible avenues must be thought out. A thoughtful leader, however, is aware of the many possible routes which a group can use to arrive at a set point and which will be most productive for the group as it travels.

(7) If you have a great deal of material to cover in the text book, decide what material the students must have, what part of the background is necessary at that age level, and what part can just be skimmed or skipped.

3. THE ATMOSPHERE TO BE CREATED

It has often been said that the education of adolescents depends on the atmosphere of the classroom. In fact, adolescence is an age when words penetrate only through the medium of an atmosphere, that condition or climate of the group which can cause frost or warmth. With boys it should be the climate where the call to greatness and values exist, where there is a bond of solidarity. For girls it is friendship, security, a common drive for values. Quite unconsciously, the atmosphere of a group crystallizes around one or other of its members who, everyone is aware, sets the standards which each wants. In both cases the group also wants an atmosphere of spontaneity and freedom consonant with its age level.

In order to nurture this atmosphere, the teacher might profit from the following rules of thumb:

—At the beginning of the year attach the greatest importance to making *contact* with the group in a balance of friendship and authority, the two being indispensable. Too many teachers have been shipwrecked by emphasizing one or the other.

—*Dialogue* with the *leaders* of the class, giving them some responsibility for the whole group.

—Arrange to know the class in some *informal* way, for example in outings, meetings before and after class, perhaps a free class discussion about the teacher and the students as persons, in order to give the students an opportunity to reveal their true personalities in another or different climate which is freer and more spontaneous. This is exceptionally difficult, in some circumstances, but extremely important. Some ingenuity on the part of the teacher is required, but the personal contact in an informal and spontaneous manner with the group should be sought.

What does the teacher do when the entire class resists religious education?

Two situations may possibly arise:

—The group resists because the structures and rules of the school or Confraternity program make the teacher follow a program which does not sufficiently take into account the questions and interests of the group.

—At a given moment the group could be saturated with religion and has had its fill of hearing about Jesus Christ.

(1) In the case in which the *structures and the rules* of the school oblige a teacher to follow a rigid and precise program, at times controlled by an examination, the teacher must do all that he can so that the adolescents for whom he is responsible can be free, free to study what will be most fruitful for them. With them he will work out a program which appeals to the best in them and will bring out the best in them.

In practice, the teacher will ask the authorities to give him the freedom to work out a more flexible program which coincides more with the questions and interests of his class. The teacher could put it this way: I think I am unfaithful to Jesus Christ if I force material on the students which they do not want. Did not Christ take a very profound account of the needs of the men with whom He conversed?

This is not an easy decision for teacher or administrator. Many factors are involved and much honesty is required on both sides of the problem. Resistance to the program can also rest in the teacher or his methods. Moreover, administrators are not always open to change, especially if they are not aware of the adolescent mind or emerging catechetical thinking. Some teachers are so attuned to adolescents that they misread the signs and over-identify with students. A situation such as this calls for consultation and discussion, possibly with other teachers in the same grade level. Then the teacher should pursue his ideas.

(2) In the case in which the group is *satiated* with everything that touches on the religious area, a teacher should probe the group to get them to explain their aversion. Why does Christ seem so annoying and difficult to understand or appreciate? In a climate of research and common reflection, the teacher should be open to their views and seek to explore with them the problem of the image of Christ and the Church before proceeding to bore or antagonize them any further.

If the reason for saturation is related to an excess of religious activities, Masses, lessons, and prayers, all imposed by the rules of the school, the teacher should work with his students and the administration in arriving at a climate of dialogue and understanding. To side with the students automatically is to be false to the situation until the whole situation is known and explored. To ignore the students, on the other hand, is to ignore the real situation of their religious growth which needs counsel and sympathetic direction at this point.

4. THE WORK OF THE TEACHER

(1) Many manuals and teacher's guides present key phrases, carefully detailed procedures, directions, and suggestions. *Must each teacher use these things as they are?*

We think not, and it is important to stress here that the teacher who is too faithful to the letter of another's lesson risks losing sight of his own gifts in the individual catechetical situation. The teacher must rethink and reshape any given plan or outlines to his class and in terms of his own insights and gifts.

(2) *The teacher must know his own teaching skills in order to discover how to approach a class in religious education.*

Whatever his particular genius, the teacher must be, before everything else, a teacher of the faith for adolescents.

(a) One of the teacher's primary concerns, then, will be to structure the material of the faith for the mind of the student. He will define and describe the outline of the faith, give exact formulations, and help the student to see beneath the images he has. He will make his teaching clear, precise, organized, and interesting.

(b) Another teacher may be primarily concerned to awaken the heart, to arouse the emerging person. Sensitive to the potential in his students, he knows how to pose questions, to share work, to speak the words that lead students to the knowledge of the truth.[4]

3. *The teacher has both limitations and gifts.*

(a) Each teacher should attempt to work in that area of religious education which best suits his temperament and aptitude. Perhaps it would be good to make known to those responsible

[4] In these two approaches, there is a way of announcing the Message which partakes of the prophet style.

On the one hand, the prophet immediately seizes earthly realities in their relationship with the mystery which he has to reveal. For him, facts and images of life are vehicles of the spiritual. The power of communion in these realities leads him to share them with the group.

On the other hand, in the communication of this to the group, he announces the Message with a power of conviction (be it in affirmation or in asking suggestive questions) which is a sign of adhesion of the truth which he reveals. He is a witness of what he announces, leading the class in its turn to adhere to the Message. It seems that every teacher must be more or less a prophet in his enunciation of the Word, and this according to his charism.

for the religion programs where our abilities lie so that, if possible, they can place us where we can grow and at the same time render the best service to the Church.

(b) The teacher should try to become versatile, capable of many approaches in religious education; but he must always start from his own individuality. For example, one who is at ease in the more formal teaching approach should not try to get involved in group discussion. First he should perfect his own approach, aiming at a more and more interesting presentation, one that is clear and related to the life around him. Then, when he has a good hold on this personal style and feels secure in his relationship with the class, he can open himself to other methods.

4. *The effect of the teacher's limitations on his work.*

The teacher must not feel that he alone is responsible for the complete education of his students in the faith. Even if he is very qualified and has great sensitivity for adolescents, it is normal that he call in others from the Christian community to complement his work.[5]

When a teacher realizes his limitations, and if he knows that he is limited mainly to one approach, he should appeal for the assistance which the Christian community can offer him. What he cannot do himself, let him give to others. Let him invite before his class a layman, a priest, a sister competent to speak to his students in some specialized area. It is fully in keeping with

[5] Murphy, "Guide for Catechists," p. 48.

Specific Guides on Speakers and Group Experiences:

(1) Such "aids" require planning and imagination, but can be invaluable aid in the formation of students.

(2) Some manuals already include introducing married couples as speakers in marriage courses. This is good, but it does not limit the field. For example, in

his role when, on a topic outside of his range and ability, he is able to benefit his group by sources within the community. He fails in his mission, however, if he becomes rigid and inflexible, holding to only one approach to the faith. An integrated education in the faith demands that the many ways of God through different persons and approaches be respected.

---

discussing the meaning of the Church and the community in a middle-class, white, suburban area, one teacher invited a Sister who worked in a slum area with migrant and immigrant groups to speak to the students. The effect was amazing; the topic of the Church and the community took on new dimension. The students visited the community and became involved in another meaning of the idea of community.

(3) An opportunity for the students to experience what they discuss is necessary, e.g., one class, within certain limits, planned a Mass with the celebrant and the teacher in terms of degree of participation, hymns, the meal afterwards. Another class planned a party for a group from a local orphanage; another class had a paschal meal.

(4) If any such aids are to be effective, careful planning is required. Speakers should fit into the overall program and be cleared with the administration; the class should be prepared to receive a speaker or a special program.

III.

THE ADOLESCENTS' THINKING

THE analysis of mentality involves a written questionnaire given to the class in order to discover the group's religious thinking on a precise point of revealed doctrine. This is followed by reflection on the teacher's part to the replies in the questionnaire in order to develop a significant approach to the religious education of his class.

When it is a matter of a small group of youths, the teacher can usually enter into dialogue with them by personal contact and through that know what they are thinking. The use of a formal analysis, however, gives him an instrument which is more technical and suitable for going into that thinking not revealed in the average day-to-day encounter. Also, at the beginning of the semester the teacher has not yet always had time for creating a climate of openness and dialogue. With larger groups or several classes, the advantages and effectiveness of this method are easier to understand. In the CCD structure there are manuals which give pre-testing on religious background. While these can be valuable, they often do not go into attitudes or basic thinking, but are restricted to technical knowledge.

1. THE RELIGIOUS VALUE OF THIS TECHNIQUE

For one thing, an analysis of mentality continues in its own way the process of incarnation adopted by God in relation to man. Like God, the teacher through the analysis enters into communion with his group; through his understanding gained from this analysis, he incarnates himself, after the divine model, into the human experience lived by the adolescent and expressed in this particular form.

Also, it is through and from this analysis that the students themselves, as at Pentecost, will be able to hear and recognize the Message, "each one in his own language." From then on, the adolescent can feel himself accepted and understood in his language, his hopes, his very being. He will know himself to be heard, understood, recognized, and loved as unique. He may be ready, then, to enter into communion with the teacher who announces the Message to him, and he may be opened personally to the Word of God.

These may seem like exaggerated claims and promises for this technique. Perhaps they are; yet it must be tried and tested and experimented with. Too frequently, adult teachers cut themselves off from the thinking of their students and simply presume that they understand and are understood by the students. A continuing dialogue provides the best conversation with another. Even friends of long standing have to rediscover the other if there has not been enough communication.

Some teachers, of course, have a degree of openness and rapport that is enviable; yet even they profit from their attitude, especially today when each new class seems to develop its own language and thinking. Many excellent teachers are rediscovering their faith and its terminology because they are listening to and being challenged by students. An analysis of mentality can be invaluable because it will speed up our common search for truth and areas of meaningful need and discussion.

2. THE PURPOSE OF THIS TECHNIQUE

(1) The analysis of mentality should reveal to the teacher the *adolescent's thinking and language* related to the Message of Christ. From this he can learn how to reach his students most effectively with the Good News.

For example, in what language or what form will the students most clearly understand the meaning of sacrament? The teacher can use the standard definition: a sacrament is a visible sign instituted by Christ to give grace. For the teacher this is appealing since it includes the approach of cause and effect, meets the theological requirements, and is meaningful to the teacher himself. He runs the risk, however, of making a sacrament something unrelated to the adolescent's world, something expressed in terms that are not alive. A student's interpretation of this definition might come out in this fashion: the sacraments are mysterious devices, distributors of something called grace.

If, however, I can discover and understand the language and needs of our students today, I might see the need for describing the sacraments as saving acts which Jesus Christ does for me today through His Church.

(2) The analysis of mentality can reveal to the teacher *the daily experiences of today's youth,* and it will be starting from these that he will lead them to enter explicitly into the realities of the faith.

For example, if I wish to speak to them of the sacrament of the sick, it is important to know in what human experience, already caught up in grace, the class has lived the situation of the sick person crushed by illness and comforted by the visit of the Lord. Perhaps one or another of the students has already seen the peace and serenity on the face of a sick relative which comes from the sacrament.

Also, the reality of sacramental grace is often experienced by adolescents in an implicit and personal manner which can be valuable to the teacher's approach. At times of great discouragement or revolt, shattered by a setback or emotional disillusionment, perhaps a friend has taken him by the arm and asked him to go to the movies, to talk something over. Suddenly the adolescent is revived because he has known that he is loved.

It is in understanding what the adolescent experiences and how he understands his own experiences that the teacher can approach the work of religious education.

(3) The analysis of mentality can reveal the areas of *special appeal or repulsion in the presentation of spiritual reality*. If we have to open them to the dimensions of Christian freedom, we might well define it as a "power of choice"; but adolescents are not necessarily sensitive to this thinking. In their view, they experience freedom as "creative power"; they feel themselves to be free when they can make their mark on things, and especially on their own lives. It will be, then, in understanding and know-

ing their line of vision that the teacher can begin to bring them to an understanding of freedom and the Good News.

It is well to note that some of our students are so repelled by certain phrases and modes of thought that we can almost speak of their being allergic to them. There will be no true religious education until this problem is seen and understood and solved in some way.

For example, regarding Christian vocation, adolescents perhaps think to themselves: If God calls me, I'm only a pawn or a tool; I am no longer free. To help them overcome this attitude the teacher must first of all know that this is what they think. The analysis of mentality is for this purpose: to give the teacher this information, in order to know what the student is really thinking as he tries to open to him the truth.

3. HOW TO SET UP THE QUESTIONNAIRE

1. *General Guides*

—Do not multiply questions; if there are too many, they may become meaningless and dull.

—Vary the types of questions so as to search out the different forms of thinking.

—Make the questions lively, simple, provocative. They should prod and stimulate curiosity.

—There are many areas which you may want to cover in this questionnaire. First decide on your topic or topics. Do you want general attitudes or information or are you interested in specific areas? If you know your group well, you may need information on specific areas. If you are uncertain about their general thinking, you may need to ask some general questions covering basic attitudes on God, the Church, the sacraments. How the areas are structured is of critical importance to the outcome of our religious instruction.

2. *Five Major Types of Questions*

A. THE DIRECT QUESTION, ORDINARY IN APPEARANCE

Example: For you, what is God? (And not: Who is God?)

This question gets to the heart of the matter, but in a general and innocuous formula which enables it to be understood by everyone. Intentionally neutral, it does not lead to a specified answer, and leaves each one free to express his own, possibly profound, feelings.

This type of question should always be placed at the beginning of the questionnaire, since it should be assured of a special hearing and answer.

B. THE PRECISE OBJECTIVE QUESTION

This type of question bears on a very circumscribed point of doctrine, or the meaning of a term, or the explanation of the meaning of one of the mysteries of the faith. It can take the form of a multiple choice, fill-in, true or false, or even matching. This form of question will do little more than furnish fragmentary and superficial information and will not reveal the deeper thought processes of the adolescent. Still, it will reveal the objective content of the religious knowledge of the class. The teacher will beware of overuse.

C. THE PROJECTIVE QUESTION

The opposite of the preceding, this question aims at sounding the depths of the students' attitudes. But it aims at achieving this in an indirect manner, by leading the students to project their most personal reactions onto other persons placed before them.

Example: In your opinion, why do so many young people find it difficult to go to confession?

At first glance, the student who is answering does not seem to be involved here. But, in fact, when he gives the reason behind the attitudes of his friends, he often gives his own reactions. The answers here are going to be difficult to interpret; you will always have to be asking yourself what is objective reporting and what are subjective views from your own students.

D. THE QUESTION STARTING FROM A LIVED OR IMAGINED SITUATION

This type of question is related to the preceding and its intention is the same.

Example 1 (questions used in preparing for a unit on the sacrament of the sick):

Imagine that you find yourself in the following situation: the night before an examination which will decide your future you are involved in an automobile accident. Laid up for a month, you find it impossible to take the examination. What will be your reaction? What kind of visit would please you?

Stimulated by this situation, hopefully the adolescent could give his true reactions and feelings. The teacher can obtain the same result in other areas by taking situations parallel to the spiritual realities but stated only implicitly, which will reveal the students' attitudes.

Example 2 (questions used in preparation for a unit on Christ):

—Without Jesus Christ, life would have no meaning.

—I would be relieved if Jesus Christ had not existed.

—Jesus Christ is very fine, but you can neither see nor touch Him; I myself have need of a human presence.

—Jesus Christ and the demands of the Gospel were all right for the first centuries of Christianity, but are no longer possible today. Do you agree or not? Why?

E. VOCABULARY QUESTIONS

Example: Here are three words—supernatural, angelic, spiritual. Tell in one line each what they immediately suggest to you.

This type of question shows what meaning the students attach to words which are common, yet ambiguous or capable of wider connotations today. This can reveal the student's own reactions to words that are commonly used in religious education.

4. PREPARING THE STUDENTS FOR THE QUESTIONNAIRE

The reactions of the group, and therefore the quality and truthfulness of the answers, depend in large measure on the manner in which the questionnaire is presented.

If the teacher who proposes it is sympathetic to the class, and knows how to prepare the ground, he can make the group amenable to the form of collaboration, and obtain their agreement. "I know you want to improve your religion classes. You would like to take a more active role. To prepare for these classes, I need you, and I ask this of you as a service."

If the questionnaire has not been prepared by the teacher himself, but is taken from some outside source, it still needs the teacher's personal endorsement and appeal to the students.

In either case, the teacher must personally introduce the material. For example, the teacher could present a questionnaire on Christ in the following way:

"If Jesus Christ were to speak to the men of today, He would not use the same words He used twenty centuries ago. He would speak to them in a living and personal way, taking up their actual problems and hopes; He would appeal to human values which concerned them; He would pay attention also to the sins of today.

"So as not to betray the thought of Jesus Christ, your teachers want to know how you today stand with regard to Him and how you speak of Him. You are asked to help in answering this questionnaire."

If it happens that a class is cool towards the questionnaire and is, perhaps, allergic to these methods of research, you might have to begin to help them change. Give some time to showing them how religious education received passively from the teacher will remain far removed from their life. (Generally, students are not adverse to such items as opinion polls. In many cases, they are fascinated by them and use them in their school newspapers.)

What they must sense here is that this questionnaire is not just an opinion-taking device, but an exploratory help for themselves and the class which will help them to grow.

Perhaps you can put it to your students somewhat in this fashion: "The Word of God is not like a meteorite fallen haphazardly in the middle of a field. It will mean nothing if it is not a response to your own important questions. It is for you first of all to speak, to express your thoughts and your needs."

The teacher also must be quite clear that the student is free, completely free, to answer or not. He does not have to put his name down and his answers will not be identifiable, unless the student expresses a desire to the contrary.

Finally, choose the most favorable time—not at the end of the year, nor during time of academic pressure. Decide whether you want it done at home, at school, at a CCD session. Depending on the length and type of answer, it might be profitable in some cases to do it in class so that you are sure of getting the answers back.

5. ANALYSIS OF THE QUESTIONNAIRE

First step: statistical count of the most frequent words and notions.

The teacher could begin his analysis by underlining the most frequently used words with a colored pencil or by noting down the key phrases, that is, those which express the mentality of the class. This involves going through each questionnaire point by point.

Done without any preconceived notions, this first reading will actually effect a kind of immersing of the teacher into the thought of the students, bringing into being very frequently a certain knowledge or insight by openness of contact. After a first impression which is sometimes deceptive, like that of entering into an early morning mist, the teacher will begin to see certain lines of force emerging, while at the same time he is asking himself about the meaning of such and such a word.

Second step: setting out the precise meaning of key words and phrases.

Several methods can be used. Most often the meaning of a word becomes clear from its context; one can apply the law of associations: what is the term which precedes this or that word; what is the word or idea which follows?

It will be good, as a general rule, to keep in mind the background of your students, the socio-economic-cultural picture that you know. Also keep in mind the thinking of the school, the local milieu.

Finally, to understand certain ambiguous expressions, the teacher may have to go to the students themselves, perhaps to a small group whose insights into the answers may be extremely interesting and enlightening.[1]

[1] In the course of speaking about the analysis of mentality, it was noted that it would sometimes be good to refer to socio-psychological data for the better understanding of the meaning attached by the adolescents to certain words and current expressions. Recourse to psychoanalytical data could also be valuable.

But it seems that an exchange with the students, in the form of a debate or a discussion with the group, could give the teacher the information which he would need for an objective reading of the answers to the questionnaire, and not only for the clarification of certain ambiguous terms or enigmatic formulas. For if an analysis of mentality can give the lines of sensitivity of the adolescents,

Third step: understanding the answers in terms of the religion program.

This step is obviously the most important and, at the same time, the most difficult. Many teachers actually refuse to take this step, content with the purely statistical data which one uses superficially.

For example, if the questionnaire is on the last things, death, it may appear that the adolescents express themselves in a way different from adults. There is a shift of emphasis. Death is not

---

it is not itself sufficient and it would be a pity to base oneself entirely on its result.

The analysis of mentality has need of being enriched by more direct contacts, more personal contacts. For example, after an investigation of freedom, the teacher asks a small group to get together to discuss it. In this discussion certain words and expressions are clarified. Further, the teacher has noticed the way in which the students approach the question, what new elements they contribute, what meaning underlies the words they are currently using, things not given in the answers to the questionnaire.

A person does not say everything in writing. There are deep realities which are difficult to formulate. In an open exchange, the students who know themselves well will be more easily led to say what they think. Further, the presence of friends, the confrontation of ideas and the contribution of experiences often leads to the emergence from oneself of a particular aspect of reality which one would have had great difficulty in putting into the answer on the questionnaire. The exchange also leads to the justification of such and such an affirmation, etc.

Finally, it should be noted that there are students who do not like to answer questionnaires but who are open to exchanges with friends of their own age. When one compares an analysis of mentality made in an academic high school situation with that of a CCD program in an inner city program, one is struck by the difference in expression. With the one group, a greater facility in editing their thought; with the other, a briefer and perhaps less easily written approach. In such a situation, discussion may be of more help.

The two methods, analysis of mentality and group discussion, complement each other.

the separation of body and soul; more, it is a check on their desire to live indefinitely.

I may have to ask myself, then, the difficult question: How do I make the link between the adolscents' insatiable wish to live and the call of God to enter into the passion, death, resurrection, and ascension of His Son, into the paschal mystery? I must understand and accept the adolescents' views on life and death in order to help my students see their own need of life and the need for man to die with Christ.

Thus, knowing and accepting the students' views on life, and using their own words and phrases, I will open to them the ineffable mystery of salvation which goes through death to a life which surpasses every expectation and hope.

6. USE OF THE RESULTS IN RELIGION CLASS

1. *As Class Preparation*

The teacher will work out his class preparation in line with those areas that the students are most sensitive to, taking as his starting point the areas to which they are most allergic or most open. He will make use of adolescent expressions and thinking insofar as they are common to all the students.

2. *With the Class Itself*

It would be good to present the results of the questionnaire, not just out of a statistical concern, but also to create ties with the class. In his presentation, the teacher should underline the positive elements in the answers, in an authentic spirit of love which knows how to discern and accept every value, even if the formulations of the values are incomplete and awkward.

On the other hand, he should present the negative aspects of the answers in a very objective manner, and without appreciable commentary, leaving it to the subsequent development in class to throw light on these points.

As far as possible, the anonymity of the answers should be respected, unless, as we have said, the students desire that their points of view be revealed.

7. CONCLUSION

The analysis of mentality is not only an instrument of investigation. More profoundly, it is a preamble to the announcing of the Word of God. Always when God speaks, He begins by awakening an expectation in the heart of man. The teacher will have to know what the expectations are in the hearts of his students that are to be awakened. Then, perhaps, the students will be open to look for God's offers.

IV.

POINT OF VIEW AND POINT OF DEPARTURE

MANY teachers find it quite easy to establish a basic point of view for the course of study and also know how to get the program off the ground. Their own procedures and insights have something of the spontaneous about them. But there are other teachers for whom this problem is a major one, solvable only after a long apprenticeship.

As we have said before, the essential condition for the approach used in this book is that the teacher be incarnated in his group. In fact, we can only speak of religious education insofar as there exists a link, a real bond, between the Message and the class: and this link is to be discovered, reflected on, and expressed by the teacher.[1]

The teacher must, first of all, discover how the message he

[1] Example: Having prepared a unit or class on the Ascension for a group of students confined to a hospital, the teacher might begin by asking: "What could this mystery of the Ascension do for those who are ill? What can this do for me as I struggle with all the problems of adult existence? What are you doing for us now, Lord? Why are you in heaven? What good is your Ascension? What did your departure mean for your Apostles? How are we, in our turn, affected and concerned by this mystery; how does it now contain our Redemption?

In this very simple example one can see how, together and immediately, the wants to express is linked to the group; but, also, he must discover how he is included in this link between the Message and his class. The first condition for his announcing any mystery of salvation is that he have first experienced a deep bond of destiny with his class in the presence of God's initiative towards man.

1. USING OR DEVELOPING A RELIGIOUS EDUCATION PROGRAM

(1) Whether a teacher opens up to a prepared course of study or is planning his own,[2] the first thing to consider is a point of view, a basic approach or particular aspect which is meaningful, which concerns the class and the teacher. We will call this the basic point of view of the program. It is this which will be the focal point of everything we have to say; it is this which gives unity to all the elements and techniques; it is like our own nervous system which gives movement and direction to our own organism.

Rarely is this point of view seen clearly from the very beginning of our preparation of our program, or even when we first

---

teacher and this group find themselves placed before the Message of Christ, concerned together with the mystery, in the same way as the Apostles on the hill of the Ascension.

[2] If the teacher is planning his own course, he must consider the following:

a. What are your aims with this particular group?

b. Do you have a clear plan in mind for the semester without a regular text?

c. Can this group work well on discussion material, or other special material?

d. Does this group need some type of material so that it will have some ready source, especially if they can and will do home assignments?

e. If you are going to prepare special material, do you have the necessary time? Honesty and discipline are needed here.

read the text or teacher's manual. Gradually, as we go further and further in our preparation, we begin to perceive and understand that core which will enrich ourselves and our students.

It might be objected, of course, that textbooks are built around some basic point of view which needs only to be read by students and teachers alike in order to be evident. However, this objection does not take into account the individual teacher and his class, their particular insights and needs, the teacher's own strengths and weaknesses, the characteristics of this class. The approach of a particular year's study from some text is valuable. What is just as essential is how the teacher intends to use what he has and how he develops it. Effective teaching means a personal assimilation and understanding, an individual approach to or point of view of the material.

(2) After discovering a fundamental point of view, the teacher must discover how to start off the program, what to do to open the students to this area of study. He must find that point which makes real the bond of unity between the teacher, the student, and the Message of Christ.

This point of departure is quite different from some type of catchy device which may have value for the first moment but draws too much attention to the students themselves or to the teacher, rather than creating a union between the two and the work to be done.

2. TWO APPROACHES

We can distinguish two catechetical approaches for adolescents. They are perhaps better understood as different emphases or accentuations rather than separate forms different from one another. Both envision the conversion of the adolescent, the education of his faith. Yet, while complementary, they still have different procedures because they answer to different needs in the adolescent period.

—*The more didactic, explanatory type of teaching:*

This is used, above all, with older adolescents. They have a need for and are more capable of understanding, analyzing, explaining, formulating, resolving. It aims at the conversion of the mind.

—*The more inductive, prophetic type of teaching:*

With emphasis on concrete experience and operating at the level of values, this approach has for its object essentially the transformation of attitudes, of making one take a position, of giving an intuition of the mystery. In brief, it helps or aims at the conversion of the heart. This type of religious education is very much in keeping with the psychological development of adolescence.

1. *The Predominantly Didactic Approach*

For the more straightforward, explanatory type of teaching, the teacher can use standard themes and introductions from other texts or programs or develop one himself. There is no difficulty in borrowing from others, providing the teacher does not use the ready-made programs as a "cure-all." He must also see that the material is that which he can handle and which is adapted to his students.

All of this understood, the didactic approach can be used easily with most prepared religious programs because it demands less personal and spiritual involvement on the part of the teacher.

Preparing a unit: In working out a section on the doctrinal formula "Outside of the Church there is no salvation," what procedure should the teacher follow?

(1) *The doctrine.* First of all, the teacher must know the doctrine thoroughly, its precise points, its relevance, its difficulties.

This might seem easy to come by, but experience has shown that teachers are far from united in handling this particular topic because they have not always explored it sufficiently.

(2) *The doctrine and the students.* What is there in the theme "Outside of the Church there is no salvation" which is of interest to the students? Is it to know how Christ, who is salvation, is linked to the institutional Church? Or is it rather to know how unbelievers, who on the level of visible realities find themselves outside the institutional Church, are in some way attached to her? It is essential to know what questions the students are asking and why. These can be used as the point of departure in the preparation of the unit.

The following are, in a more general way, some questions which a teacher should consider each time he approaches a topic:

—What aspect of the doctrine is important for the students' understanding of the Christian life?

—What clarification do they actually need now?

—Which of their intellectual interests is related to this doctrine?

—What problem or question do they see in this topic?

—How could the understanding of this doctrine cause difficulties or further problems in their faith life?

After the teacher has thought out the above, he can find the starting point for a particular topic. A possible example, which considers the students in relation to the topic, might be the following, worked out around the theme "Outside of the Church there is no salvation."

You live in an area where there are many Protestants. Often you admire them for their qualities. You even say to yourselves: How is it possible that these people whom we don't meet in our Church can actually be joined to Jesus Christ? Is the phrase "Outside of the Church" incorrect? Are those people damned? This seems impossible.

(3) *Outlines and analogies.* After determining the point of view and a starting point, the teacher still must draw up the outline for the topic, or even the semester.

The outline will, of course, vary from teacher to teacher, depending on the class situation and the temperament of the teacher. Some will be able to work out a detailed progression using the group-discussion approach from topic to topic. Others will work from key images or ideas that call for direction, explanation, or exposition.

2. *The Predominantly Inductive Approach*

The inductive approach in religious education borrows less from the process of the rational intelligence since it is directed more towards the heart, the living existent person. It envisions that wider and profound education of the being which works a change; it calls for conversion. It is, we believe, the one that corresponds most to the age of puberty.

In the concrete situation of a person moving and growing before him, the teacher will feel ill at ease if he contents himself with borrowing the approach and starting point of someone else.

Why? Because this particular approach gets its convincing and converting power not from the quality or force of theoretical exposition, but from the signs and facts given through the teacher. What is stronger than witness for bringing about adherence to truth? The truth and quality of a man's life is a great source of teaching. A person is not converted except in the meeting with a sign. Hence the necessity for this type of religious education which is intimately connected with witness, which develops from a personal word (not a word borrowed from another or taken from a book) which first of all springs up from the depths of the teacher's own life and thinking.

Preparing a unit.

(1) *The Message.* In the didactic approach, we posed the question: What is the doctrine to be taught? —the word "doctrine" being used in its most intellectual sense.

In this approach we ask, instead: What is the *message* to be shared? To put it another way: What is, in the fullest sense, the meaning of the mystery in relation to the heart of man?[3]

(2) *The Message and the students.* The teacher's thinking must be oriented to his class's thinking on a topic.[4] By questioning he will try to pinpoint the adolescents' views on the message

[3] *Heart* here indicates man insofar as he desires the good.

[4] It is possible that certain teachers seek first a resonance of the mystery in their own lives and then in that of the student. There is nothing wrong with this, on the condition that the teacher also ask himself the question of the group.

to be covered, to discover what they are thinking and reacting to, what they accept or wish to reject. For example, he must ask himself:

—How does this particular part of the Good News influence the students' life of faith?

—How does it relate to their own profound needs?

—How can it become Good News for them?

—To what problems in their Christian lives does this part of the Message give an answer?

—Through what part of their thinking can they adhere to this point of Revelation, or from what part of their thinking will they reject it?

—How are they living this Message—spontaneously or implicitly?

—What experiences do they have of it?

(3) *The Message and the teacher.* After having considered the relationship between the material to be covered and the class, the teacher is still faced with a problem: In what way does a program of religious instruction which aims to develop a real assent from the students reflect and integrate the teacher's own life and witness?

If, as we know, the Word of God is inexhaustible, if its work of converting a person is never finished, then the teacher can and must make a spiritual effort so that the same Word which touches his class touches him also, questions him, and converts him.

He must ask himself the following:

—How does this aspect of Christ's message concern me?

—What does it reveal for me?

—What is to be overthrown or changed in my life by this Word coming to me in this class?

In the measure that the teacher makes the Message his own, in the measure that the doctrine comes alive in his own existence, in that measure his words will be at once doctrine and life, instruction and a call to growth for his students.

The teacher who truly loves his group will be able to identify with them so as to share in their meeting with the Message of Christ. He will make himself like someone who lets himself be seized and possessed by the truth before communicating it to others. As long as we are on earth, are we not always in a certain way involved in the same search, the same struggles, and the same hopes as our class?

3. *Complementary Aspects of the Two Approaches*

The two approaches which have just been analyzed are not to be considered as opposing systems. We must again stress their complementary meaning. In fact, it is difficult to imagine a predominantly didactic approach which would be without any relation to the faith life of the group, or a predominantly inductive approach which did not have a certain amount of structuring.

Furthermore, it can and will happen that the two approaches will be needed in the same class session, especially with the upper grades. If one has used the inductive method with a group, it is indispensable, even after an animated and rich discussion, to draw together all of the separate elements into a logical and structured synthesis. The students' study of other subject areas has accustomed them to an intellectual discipline which can and has affected their knowledge of faith; they want some kind of structure, something solid, so that they can express themselves and express to others the answers given by Revelation to man's problems which are beginning to grow in them.

Still, it is important to distinguish the two approaches because each teacher, according to his own needs and talents, will feel more at ease with one or the other.

3. WHERE TO START

It remains to discover where to start. In fact, very often as a teacher goes through the procedures just analyzed, his point of departure becomes quite obvious: a particular situation, crisis, problem becomes the evident opening.

Sometimes, however, it will not come so quickly. The teacher will have to search for it—in the magazines the students read, in their conversations, in their reactions to the world around them.

A beginning is a difficult step in any field; religious education is no exception. Students do not like to be coddled or trapped by some device into a situation they do not want. Some teachers are extremely clever in arousing interest deceptively; that is, a student gets keyed up by one discussion only to be led to some other area where he is not interested.

A good starting point requires some serious thinking, not because of its attention-getting values, but because of its relationship to what is to be covered.

If a teacher is working in a city area, he might open a unit on worship by asking about the meaning of community in the urban society. In a rural area, the idea of Church or gathering might be introduced through the notion of the students' own community life.

4. THE THEME

After one has read through and made his own the material he is working with, or has thought out and developed his own program, he should go back over the whole procedure to cut out the dead wood, to tighten up the loose ends, to clarify his own thinking. This process is a continual one throughout the year; careful and critical evaluation is needed in order to keep the theme alive to the class. Some teachers are gifted enough so that their long-range plans will hold up well; others perhaps need more practice and in the beginning should reëvaluate as they go along.

After the initial preparation the teacher should either state the theme for the first time, or restate it after the prepration process. The theme basically is the underlying reason or aim of the program, in which the teacher expresses a doctrinal reality in such a way that it meets the profound interests of the group and reveals man to himself. It is, as it were, a summary of the goals.

For example, a program on Abraham in the sophomore year is directed to adolescents who have just left the security of childhood and are uneasy at entering this new life. The point of view of the teacher is to help his students to see how God, in asking Abraham to uproot himself from his native country, was urging him towards a greater and more beautiful future. At the time spent on Abraham, this aim could be set out precisely in a theme for the students themselves: When God calls someone, it is always a call to the promised land.

The stated theme, then, aside from its value for the teacher as a terminal point for his thinking, can be, if well formulated and easy to memorize, a point of reference for the student and can sometimes open new insights for his spiritual growth.

V.

THE USE OF CONTEMPORARY EVENTS IN RELIGIOUS EDUCATION

THE daily newspapers, weekly news and picture magazines, television documentaries, and newsbroadcasts are all part of a catechist's life. Here is a reserve of useful documents, facts of life about the world or the Church. These facts, like those coming from the class's own experiences, will help the teacher discover and use the language and thinking of the adolescents and will enable him to awaken interest in or to share in the needs of the students. It should almost be automatic that the teacher would use them in his religious education program.

Two questions come to mind:

—What events should be selected and how are they to be used? As a way to get attention? As illustration or support for belief?

—How are they to be presented? Are there rules for the use and presentation of current events in religious education?

1. EVENTS: HOW TO USE THEM

We can make a double distinction: What type of event should we use, and in what manner?

1. *Types of Events*

We can consider three basic types: those of the secular world around us, those of the Church, those of our students themselves.

A. THE SECULAR WORLD

These are the events stemming from the life of the world: international news, national life, cultural events, or occurrences from everyday life. Here is one example:

A restatement of an event could be taken from a daily newspaper or television news program.

A fire breaks out in an apartment. The whole family escapes, but then it is discovered that one child has been trapped. The fire having reached the entrance, it is impossible for anyone to get back into the house.

Suddenly a window opens and a young child calls to his father. The father instructs the child to jump. Surrounded by smoke, the child answers that he can't because he can't see. The father simply cries out to him, "That doesn't matter. I can see you. Jump quickly." The child jumps and is safely caught in his father's arms.

The teacher himself must be alive to all the world and to national and even local events. In any discussion of freedom, for instance, the problem of race riots in recent years would almost have to be taken up. Or regarding man's obligation to love his fellow man, discussion of international and national assistance plans should be part of the instruction. The appearance of celebrities in the local area, the values expressed by the newspapers and movies and television programs, all are related to the world of faith where we discuss vocation, zeal, friendship, love.

B. EVENTS IN THE CHURCH

These are current happenings from the Church's life today. The teacher, of course, should be careful not just to note what the Pope or a bishop is doing; otherwise, the students may identify the Church with the hierarchy only. The stronger emphasis should be on the lives of all believers.

C. EVENTS IN THE LIVES OF THE STUDENTS

These events from the class's own experiences can be either from the secular world or the Church. They are worth treating separately because they are of more immediate concern to the students in their relations to one another. They constitute lived experiences which are privileged and whose human and Christian meaning it is necessary to discover in order to make them more fully lived and understood.

2. *The Use of Events*

There are four ways to make use any of the above events: analogy, witness, proof, illustration.

A. ANALOGY

The analogical method starts from the appeal of a human experience and leads the student towards greater truth and insight. We may, then, have analogies taken from the human and current experiences of love, friendship, fatherhood.

To be honest, it is often difficult to use analogy. Either it is badly used or else it does not quite match what the teacher wants to reveal. If analogy is to work, therefore, the event under discussion must:

—have a spiritual bearing and value;

—not be opaque in its immediate meaning, but allow passage to another level; also it is necessary that the analogy be capable of evoking an experience more or less lived by the adolescents themselves.

In the example already cited of the child jumping into the arms of the father, the adolescent should be able to come to the attitude of the believer and his relation to God, the attitude of confidence in the Word of God who calls to him, who loves him like a father and saves him. Further, at certain moments in our lives are we not like that child who has confidence in his father, so that in the crises and obscurities of faith one can have confidence in God?

B. WITNESS

Some events express the way in which the Message of salvation lives at the heart of human existence. The Good News of Jesus Christ is not something of the past, something unreal. If in the past this Good News has profoundly changed and overwhelmed the lives of men, it still possesses the power to overwhelm our contemporaries; it takes hold of the lives of men today.

C. PROOF

Some events are valuable because they verify or affirm what we believe. They provide security for our thinking. For example, the speech of Paul VI at the United Nations reaffirmed that the Message of Christ is a message of universal love and peace; the work of the laity, priests, and sisters in poverty programs can be used as a proof of the concern of the Christian community for others. We might remark, however, that some events used as proof may be helpful to our own thinking and show the truth of our beliefs; yet they can still leave the will unmoved.

D. ILLUSTRATION

The illustrative use of events helps give a concrete form to a difficult explanation, making it closer, more accessible. Many need the concrete and sensible in order to reach the abstract, the realm of the idea.

2. GUIDELINES FOR USING EVENTS

1. *The Secular World*

A. CHOOSING THE EVENTS

First rule: The event must interest the whole group.

All or at least a good number of the students should be interested in what you are presenting. If not, the teacher takes the chance of finding himself in front of a passive and uninterested group. To determine the interest, the teacher should consider:

(1) the age, scholastic background, and spiritual and cultural level of the group;

(2) using an event that the students are capable of assimilating in terms of their own spiritual and human experience and thus profiting from it. Adolescents are interested only in the measure in which they feel themselves concerned, or in the measure in which the fact offers a certain continuity with their own experience.

A discussion on the film *The Bridge on the River Kwai* in terms of man's need for values in a hostile environment may fall flat with students who are not leader- or hero-oriented, or who have not yet understood or are incapable of understanding the structures of a community.

Second rule: Do not use an event that upsets or unsettles the students.

The teacher, in his choice of contemporary events, will avoid all those which make too strong an appeal to the feelings. This appeal to the feelings can be more of an obstacle than a help to the teacher. He will, in fact, have a great deal of difficulty in going beyond the event to help the students understand the human and Christian meaning. This rule is valid for every group, but above all for groups of girls. For example, in a discussion of poverty or greed or theft, the students can get so absorbed in the actual details or causes that they are unwilling to go beyond. For example, a teacher of our acquaintance wanted to get into a discussion on the problem of wealth and poverty in religious life. An article in *Life* magazine dealing with a family that had borrowed money from a particular religious community was used, but the situation itself proved so fascinating and interesting that the teacher was unable to get to the main problem of wealth and poverty.

Third rule: The event must permit passage to the mystery, the Good News being revealed through the event.

The event must not be considered as an end in itself. In religious education, human experience is not taken in itself but in virtue of the mediation of language. It is the revealed Word which gives rise to this mediation, which makes the judgment as to the choice of this or that event according to its aptitude to translate what God says of it. In a general way we can state the following:

(1) The passage from the event to the Good News is a delicate one to make. There is sometimes an unfortunate break, a kind of leap-frog to be made in the sense that the teacher brings in Revelation in an almost brutal, disconnected fashion. At times there may be a real break with what went before (especially if what went before was presented through what might be called the *deus ex machina* approach). It is necessary to remain in continuity with the ideas in the event, while gradually and necessarily going beyond it.

(2) One of the means which facilitates the passage from an event to mystery is that of witness, by which the teacher can communicate the answer of the Church. Thus, in the question of abortion because of the possibility of a deformed child, a teacher made an appeal to the father of a family having a sick child at home, one well known to the students. The father was

able to show the inalienable value which the Church recognizes in every human being, including the sick. Every person is sacred.

B. PRESENTING THE EVENTS

Fourth rule: The events must be a part of the teacher himself when he uses them.

A certain interiorization of the event by the teacher himself is needed. For this, he must feel himself concerned in the event. The teacher, then, becomes a witness of it. In fact, the teacher must not let the event be a pretext for his teaching only. In such a case, he begins with the event but is not really interested in it; it is used so that the rest of the lesson will follow.

Using an event as a pretext is a false and abusive way of dealing with students. It can lead to a certain laziness in catechists who use techniques for their immediate and sometimes superficial value and who do not make a sufficient effort to present the Word of God in a language meaningful to the students (and therefore meaningful to the teacher). Above all, such a use of events misses the richness and the fullness of an experience. We telescope the human.

Fifth rule: The event must be given in its totality, in all its human dimensions.

The presentation of an event in its totality and all its human dimensions allows the students to take possession of it, become one with it, go to the heart of the matter. After that the teacher must discover the way his students react. He should let them talk, express this own reactions, even initiate a debate. This will help the assimilation and participation by the students. Also, the teacher must be prepared to be guided by the way the students understand and analyze the event.

For example, if a teacher has brought material into class on abortion laws, he may have to be prepared to let the students open their opinions on abortion to him and to one another. What must interest the teacher is not the presentation of the ideas on the abortion reform, but the reactions to, the personal opinions given of these reforms. The teacher should avoid over-objectifying the events, of maintaining a purely objective presentation. Any event is lived by persons with their whole personality, thought processes, and personal background. Hence we cannot divorce the person and event, the student and his reaction to an event. It is in the teacher's basing his approach on the students' world and reaction that he can begin an education of the faith, announce the Word of God, and at the same time understand how the Good News can be meaningful to the needs and interests of men today.

Consequently:

(1) The teacher will be open to whatever there is of positive value in the students' reactions to the event so as to assume them himself, recognizing there the signs of God's creation and the Incarnation of Christ.

(2) The teacher will be equally aware of whatever in the students' reactions to the event is weak or contrary to the faith. The values created by God and assumed by Christ are touched by sin; sin, in fact, touches man in his relation with God and the universe.

(3) Finally, the teacher will be attuned, when possible, to the meaning of the event in terms of the future realization of the Kingdom.

Hence, in presenting and understanding an event in its fullness, the teacher must be capable of using it fully and of permitting the students to be open to its full dimension, and then be capable of extracting from it all that draws man to God and perhaps shows the weakness of man to God.

N.B. The teacher should not impose the sacred on the secular automatically. He must take care not to christianize everything; the secular or profane, in fact, has its own domain and its own end. To say too quickly that "this is Christian" even if one quickly adds "without knowing it") is to suppose unduly that a person acted with a Christian intention; it is oversimplifiction.

Also, the teacher should avoid jumping to conclusions that he sees through his *own* faith. To teach is to help another in a progressive working out of things, and thus the teacher cannot presume that his students will spontaneously see things in the way be does.

Frequently, a teacher forgets that he is that—a teacher. In his enthusiasm for the Christian meaning of a current event, he is sometimes disappointed because he seems to be the only one seeing it. He forgets two things: his own maturity and insight in the faith, and his obligation as a teacher to develop these in his students.

Sixth rule: Make the event relevant to the students.

The adolescent is, of course, more sensitive to some topics than to others. What is perhaps most important to him at this age is how a particular event relates to him. For example, in discussing an episcopal conference, the teacher, rather than going into rules, proposed agenda, attendance, and so forth, might use the event in this manner: If you had a chance to propose questions to the conference, what would they be?

2. *Events in the Church*

First rule: Keep events within the context of the whole Church. Do not isolate.

This rule is designed to show the students the coherence and permanence of the Christian attitude in the course of history. If the teacher can enlarge or generalize on an event, he helps the student to avoid a limited view of the world.

For example, the work of the Church in the inner-city movement is to be placed in relationship with the similar witnesses found in the Church: Vincent de Paul, Dorothy Day, the Josephite Fathers.

Second rule: Avoid emphasizing exceptional events or exploiting them for their own sakes.

This would be the case, for example, with conversions of famous people. There is a respect for personal decisions which does not seem to fit into wide-scale publicity. The teacher should know how to recognize and utilize the same sign in the more average individual.

Third rule: Respect the freedom of the students to accept or reject, when freedom is allowed.

This rule applies above all when it is a question of situations where the Church is involved more directly in certain events in the world—for example, strikes, or conscientious objectors. The teacher should avoid taking sides so as to avoid forcing the students to take positions which are still open. In other words, the teacher must attempt to understand and see the different and complex issues and the freedom of choice involved. This does not rule out an objective presentation of the Church's teaching in the formation of Christian judgment. But in face of such complex issues, which do not always have a simply arrived at answer, it will be good to question with and to search with the students. It is in dialogue in which each one has his own position that the teacher will avoid seeming to be a domineering know-it-all.

In some extremely sensitive and difficult areas, it may be necessary to leave the event or to reflect on another analogous situation. On the role of Pope Pius XII and the Jews, for instance, the teacher might help the class become aware of the difficulties experienced by great men of state in the making of decisions in serious circumstances. The teacher might offer such and such a drama of conscience in the life of a well-known person. If this procedure does not resolve the problem which has been raised, it will at least cool the debate and permit a deeper understanding of the event.

Fourth rule: Proceed rapidly to the Message of Christ.

Starting from some event in the Church, the teacher should not delay in relating it to Christ's Message in order to show the full meaning of the event, seen now in the light of the whole of Revelation, including that of the Old Testament. What Karl Rahner writes about the reading of facts and events in the world is true also, *a fortiori* one could say, of facts and events in the life of the Church:

> It may be, indeed it is certain, that it is possible to read the message of Jesus Christ with any clarity and fullness in the book of the world only if it has first been read in the book of the Scriptures.[1]

[1] Rahner, *op. cit.*, p. 71.

Thus, if we speak of racial segregation, of the attitudes of those Christians who oppose integration in school or neighborhood, we should make reference to the words and actions of Christ. But the attitude of Christ will be fully revealing of the total plan of God only if they are seen in terms of certain texts of the Old Testament on welcoming and accepting the stranger, and also in terms of the witness of people in the history of the Church. Similarly, the trip of Pope Paul VI to India will be understood most clearly in the context of the total revelation of God: the desire of God that the unity of the human community be centered around Christ; the call to peace from God; His call to us to love the weak and the poor (cf. the message of the great prophets).

N.B. Reference to the Old Testament and to the tradition of the Church involves risking that the answer given to students appear dull to them. The teacher must know his students and their reaction to the use of Scripture and history.

Also, all of these approaches in religious education based on contemporary events suggested either by the students or by the teacher could be used at the beginning of a more explicitly structured catechesis to be given at a later time.

3. CONCLUSION

(1) A religious-education program based totally on contemporary events will not be sufficient to educate totally the adolescents' faith. All of these current events do not necessarily present the occasion for the presentation of the whole Revelation. We can-

not force life or read into it so as to make the whole Message of Christ emerge from it and from it alone.

(2) Faith (which is capable of clarifying all dimensions of human life) gives life with what it reveals from on high. At the same time that we work to show the incidence of faith in the existence of man, it is necessary that we take care to reveal the design of God: while faith is revealed and realized in man, it remains transcendent and of divine initiative.

This demands in practice that the teacher give, as often as possible, an organic and substantial presentation of the faith as it is contained in Scripture, tradition, and synthesized in the creeds. This is to work towards a coherent religious instruction, even though the forms and approaches vary according to groups, ages, and special situations. It is thus becoming more and more apparent that a teacher needs to be thoroughly knowledgeable about the religious and educational psychology of adolescents. That is why, also, the teacher must be careful to arrange strongly spiritual events such as retreats, days of friendship and reflection, opportunities for sharing in the Eucharist. For in such as these the student can be brought to the awareness of the transcendence of God as well as to the immanence of Him in his brothers.

(3) For all that, the Christian education of outlook on the world has a proper place in the religious formation of adolescents. To forge a link between their life and the faith is to give them a Christian vision of their experiences and situations as they make their way to the Kingdom of God.

VI.

STUDENTS' QUESTIONS

1. IMPORTANCE OF STUDENTS' QUESTIONS IN RELIGIOUS EDUCATION

Often, it is to be hoped, in the course of a class adolescents ask questions: some are pertinent, others are off the point, some give the impression of being time-killers. Should the teacher stop for them? Should the teacher provoke questions? What questions should be answered? And how important are the answers?

Computers cannot ask questions. Only man can question. And the more one reflects on the way man understands, the more one regards the importance of students' questions in the discovery and deepening of Revelation.

1. *On the Natural Level*

The psychologist John Dewey has shown us the value of questioning in his analysis of the act of knowing: the first step in understanding consists in asking oneself a question. One could even add: a person truly understands only to the extent to which the mind poses questions to itself. Such an affirmation should make us think more about the value of religious education which emphasizes the role of the teacher predominantly or exclusively as a lecturer.

Further, for many people the asking of a question is the first step in making oneself heard, the first step in self-expression. In this sense it could be the first expression of one's freedom. How many adolescents there are who appreciate the one who helps them free themselves from timidity by leading them in a friendly way to ask questions. How unfortunate, on the other hand, are those students in a school or CCD program where they feel that they have no right at all to a word.

Needless to say, then, there is quite a problem when a teacher is incapable of stimulating questions or encouraging a search for truth within the group. What can come as a result is a discipline problem which really represents the students' need for some type of expression.

Finally, questions also have a social importance. To ask a question is to commit oneself before the others; it is to take a position in such a way that one will be obliged to hold one's ground; it is to sustain one's challenge, which the question represents, and not to withdraw in the face of the answer.

2. *On the Level of Faith*

Have you noticed how often Christ spoke or acted only after demands or questions? From the first disciples who came to follow Him He heard these words: "Master, where do you live; where do you come from?" Sometimes, He Himself provoked the questions in His disciples or in the people He met. At the time of the healing of the man born blind, for example, Jesus did not truly ask the question before the miracle, but after. He accomplished the miracle with such quiet simplicity that the one cured began to ask questions of Him. It was after the miracle, in fact, that the question arose and it was at that moment that Jesus revealed Himself.

Jesus knows the depths of men's hearts. He knows that no one can welcome the Good News unless the Father draws him, that the light of the Holy Spirit must be within the person. It is this delicate action of the Holy Spirit which first reveals itself before Revelation in the form of a humble search, an unrest, and finally by a question which rises to the surface of the consciousness. "You would not have sought me if you had not already found me." Is not a question the sign of the Holy Spirit's action in the depths of the questioner? And the more a man is led by the Spirit, the more he will ask true questions.

2. THE TEACHER'S ATTITUDE

Ordinarily, when a student asks a question, the first thought of the teacher will be to grasp the sense of the question quickly and to answer it with the least possible delay. He does not want to be caught unawares, and he wishes to reply as well as possible.

More important, however, than giving the impression of unbeatable competence in his field is the teacher's attitude towards questions. Basically, he should welcome them, be open to questions; even more, he must direct his attention to the quality of the question itself and its full meaning in terms of the questioner. He must be convinced that the essential issue is not the speed and accuracy of his answer, as if he were duplicating a computer. More, let him appear in the eyes of his students as the one who knows how to be silent in order to listen, as someone who seeks to understand before speaking, as a person who takes the adolescent seriously in his questioning state. The best answer will be that one which the student has sensed to have been born and arisen from the depth of the person questioned.

This approach is at the root of all authentic dialogue, supposing a certain renunciation of the instinctive need to make ourselves secure by giving a good answer quickly. A climate of dialogue which allows a truer communion in the question of a young person is what is important. A spirit of welcome on the part of the teacher will enable him better to understand this approach.

3. WHAT QUESTIONS TO ANSWER

Students who are at ease with a teacher and the class will offer innumerable questions. Must they all be answered?

Any teacher wishing to answer all of the students' questions will quickly lose control over the class. A primary rule for classifying questions to which an answer must be given and which should be ignored or rejected is: *Stop only for those questions which have or can have an interest for the majority of the group and whose answers will help the students advance more fully in their search for truth.*

(1) The teacher owes it to himself to know his students well enough to pick out the questions that are really meaningful.

He must set aside, however, certain questions which are too individualistic or too far off the topic at a particular time.

(2) He should train the students to ask questions which interest the whole class. Some precise rules for class questioning are:

(a) Never ask a question that does not interest the whole group.

(b) The question must take account of the person to whom it is addressed.

(c) It is forbidden to think out loud. Before asking a question, think it out.

(3) The teacher must know how to limit questions, especially if they are off the subject; otherwise he runs the risk of sabotaging the plan worked out for the group. Also, he should not go back too often and for any length of time to certain subjects, such as freedom, faith, and so on, even if the students keep questioning. Frequently, their interest becomes purely speculative and the students are no longer personally involved in the topics.

(4) When a student asks a question which the teacher regards as important, but off the topic, there are two ways of answering it:

(a) The question is for the whole group and the teacher is prepared to answer. He should preface his answer with the remark that although this question does not fit into the program, he is going to answer it since it concerns the whole class. He must then involve the entire class in discovering the answer and try to clarify the problem that has been raised as well as possible.

(b) The class is not ready for this particular question and the teacher must reject it, pointing out that the question is too far removed from the subject matter and that the answer itself would not be necessary for the group. He could, of course, offer to answer the question later to the particular individual or any others interested.

(c) Perhaps there is too little time to handle the question well, or the teacher is not prepared to answer it. He should tell them that he will take up the question later after he has prepared for it.

Finally, and this may take considerable practice, the teacher should know how to maintain a certain balance between the individual student and the class, between attention to the person and the need of the whole group, and between the subject under consideration and the questions that arise from it.

4. FINDING AND EXPRESSING THE REAL QUESTIONS

Adolescents have difficulty in expressing their problems. When they do, frequently it is in language incomprehensible to the class and the teacher. The teacher should, first of all, train students to formulate and deliver questions in a precise and clear fashion, but also develop in students a capacity for real attention and listening to others. In the measure that the teacher is demanding on these two points, the group will function well as a group.

1. *Create an Accepting Atmosphere*

It is essential that the teacher know how to evoke a climate of sympathy and friendship. Students too often are prisoners of their own personal problems to be capable of truly listening to each other. The teacher must be constantly concerned about leading the students out of themselves so that they can enter into a true dialogue. They cannot really express themselves until they feel supported by the group and really listened to. Even the most timid among them must be able to feel himself enough at ease so as to be able to speak. Each student has a right to speak.

But we must also know how to keep silent so as to listen. It is just as important to be attentive to the other in silence as it is to be able finally to express oneself with ease and simplicity. The students must be taught to know each other, to consider and understand the other by really listening to him as he is. The welcoming of the thinking of another is the sign of the friendship one has for him.

2. *Stress What is Valuable in a Question*

The teacher, especially at the beginning of a semester, may have to restate the student's question, to disengage the true meaning of it when it is proposed with some vagueness or awkwardness. He should bring out its cogency, keeping everything in it that is valuable and original, and help the class see its full meaning.

The best manner of enhancing a question is to propose it to the class in another light, translating what the student wanted to say in a language clearer and closer to the interests of the group.

3. *Ask for an Explanation*

The teacher can also help to delineate the question more precisely by: (a) asking the meaning of a word used by the student—"What do you mean by . . . ?"; (b) asking for a more detailed explanation—"What do you intend here. . . . ?"; (c) asking for an illustration—"Could you given an example, a fact . . . ?"

Often this explanation and exchange help the class understand the question. At the same time that the teacher is asking the student to describe the concrete situation which gave rise to his question, he can also give or propose an interpretation, verifying it with the student who is speaking: "Are you trying to say that . . . ?" Eventually, the teacher himself will possibly tie together the question with the facts and analogies gathered from the exchange. Lastly, he will appeal to the class, asking one student to express the same question in other terms. If an answer is to have any meaning for a class, the question must be understood by all.

5. DISCOVER THE MEANING OF THE QUESTION

In order to answer a question properly, it is necessary that the question be formulated as clearly as possible, that the full meaning (and sometimes the underlying meaning) of the question for the student and the class be brought out.

To a group of adolescents who ask, "Why is it necessary to go to a priest to confess?", a teacher could answer, "Man is so made that he has need of a sign to be assured of the pardon of his sins." This is an answer. But perhaps it came too quickly? Has the real question been answered?

(1) Quite easily, a teacher can risk missing the essential problem. Actually, what is the question on the lips of a student?

In the abstract, or perhaps in a text book, the question contains only what is expressed. Here, on the contrary, it carries an existential burden; it is rooted in a personal history and arises from an interior universe where it has taken a body. What is hidden behind the same words which another might have said; what are its deep motivations? Nothing is more difficult or more exhausting than to try to hear this universe of realities underlying every question. What is expressed in the question is less important than that which it wishes to say.

"Can not a person obtain pardon for one's sins without confessing them to a priest?" In discussion with a group of adolescents, the psychological implications of this question on the level of the family might be revealed: an unconscious identification between the priest and the "father," an authority against which the students are already in revolt. How would it be possible to give a valid answer to the question without first coming to grips with and solving the problem of paternal authority?

What can be done, then, in order to understand a question in depth? The teacher will be handicapped if he is not in tune with the mental and emotional world of the adolescents, a world which they often express very badly. Studies of group dynamics have shown just how far people can be from one another in dialogue; one often has a dialogue of the deaf. Because individuals have a vocabulary which is more or less personal, one knows very little of what the other is thinking. Sometimes a person ends up by hearing only himself.

To understand a question well, therefore, one must give great attention to the one who is speaking. It is a matter of love and poverty, a question of being available, of being capable of submitting everything to the other's question so as to enter into a completely different mental, intellectual, psychological, and religious universe. It is a question of discovering not only what is said but why. To find the meaning and the motivation of a question, the teacher must refer to the social context, the general thinking of the student, and especially to depth psychology which often gives the best clues.

(2) More concretely, to discover the meaning of a question, the teacher will try to relate it to one of the three great types of questions which follow:

1. *The Problem Question*

A question such as "Why does the Church oblige us to go to Mass on Sunday?" is resolved only by accurate information—participation in the Eucharist is our personal response to God who calls together all of the believers, etc. Because such a question springs from a difficulty in the order of knowing due to ignorance or insufficient knowledge, we call it a problem question.

This first type necessitates competence in the order of knowledge. If the teacher is incapable of answering at the moment, then he should simply admit his lack of knowledge and he will respond later when he has prepared an answer. All the same, adolescents expect teachers to be competent, and it would be regrettable if this delay were a regular occurrence.

2. *The Mystery Question*

This type is very difficult to grasp because of its close relationship to the very mystery of faith. When students ask, "If God is good, why does evil exist?" or "God knows everything; He knows if I am going to heaven or to hell. How am I free?", it is not enough to give an immediate proof establishing the freedom of man or the goodness of God. The question opens onto the mystery, a mystery which is the personal secret of God and which we are not going to grasp because of our insufficiency of being and love. It is in the nature of man not to be able to answer it as he would the problem question because this is not in the order of knowing but in the order of existence.

But what do you with the students when they ask these questions? Can you give them some answers?

(1) *Make the students see and experience more fully the meaning of existence.* The teacher should first know whether the student's question is the result of much thought and study. If it is, then he can attempt to help the student trace his way through the difficulties of this problem. If it is not that, but more of a face-to-face meeting with the mystery, then the teacher must be careful not to proceed with an intellectual explanation that will leave him talking to himself.

If he finds that neither he nor the group can adequately handle the introduction to the mystery, then the approach to this mystery must be found in the relationship of love and presence that the teacher has to his class. He will help the students grasp their relationship to this mystery by improving the quality of his personal relationships and also his own will to make his students exist more intensely.

The more he helps an adolescent to exist fully, to develop, to succeed, the more he helps him develop his potentialities for loving, for taking the initiative, for taking responsibility, the more he helps him to grow in his capacity for existence; and in this way the student will be better prepared to understand his own approach to this mystery question.

For example, a student who has been given the chance for personal initiative, for freedom to create, will no longer ask the same questions about freedom. In the same way, how often has it been said that a person who has been deeply loved no longer finds himself with the same attitude towards the question of evil? The experience which he has had or still has of a love which touches him personally will not have solved the question of evil on the rational level. But it will have led him, little by little, to accept evil as a dimension of existence. At least his attitude of revolt towards this mystery question will be lessened.

This presupposes, of course, that the teacher himself has truly asked these questions of himself, that he has had a similar experience of growing in his own existence, of being more, and that he has himself grown and changed in his position before these questions.

(2) *Give direction*. Sharing in the same mystery does not excuse the teacher from giving his students some orientation and direction.

Sometimes it would seem good to correct certain false motivations which lie at the base of the question. For example, the impossibility of admitting the goodness of God and the existence of hell sometimes is rooted in an Oedipus complex, that is, in unconscious resentment against a father-castrator. In other cases, the true face of God will be hidden by a whole religious imagery, by some current thinking, by objections which the student has heard or read.

Furthermore the teacher will try to promote an inner attitude of openness to the mystery and to grace by citing events, experiences of others, analogies taken from experiences of adolescents or adults which can speak to them. For answering the mystery question, ideas will not be of great help. The way of analogy and of witness will most easily help the students attain a certain depth of vision.

3. *The Delaying Question*

Finally, there are those questions which spring from a lack of interest or concern of the students, or even from the group's need for relaxation. These are the ones off the subject. Very familiar to many teachers, they can well indicate a break between the teacher's planned program and the attention and understanding of the class. They can also also show a wide gap between what the teacher is presenting and what would involve the real and valuable interests of the students.

What does the teacher do then?

This kind of question can challenge the teaching genius of anyone. He should refuse to answer it if the question is obviously a sign of a lack of interest in the topic or just a way to get off the topic. He can indicate that the question is off the topic and that it could be answered after class if anyone wants to wait.

It is important also not to give in to the temptation to answer every question. The teacher who quickly answers every question is like the doctor who prescribes only aspirin.

Generally speaking, the teacher will avoid these delaying questions by encouraging real dialogue on the program for the day and in refraining from giving an answer to all the questions which come up.

N.B. This type of question can also be a good indicator that the teacher may have to rethink his approach or program, especially if such questions are frequently asked. There are many problems involved in this situation, ranging from an individual who is having difficulty to the attitude of the entire class. Occasionally, it may be necessary to think about the need for relaxation. In any case, the teacher will have to know his class very well in order to make a decision in this area.

6. CONCLUSION

For the convenience of analysis, we have used three major types of questions. But this is not a rigid distinction. Sometimes a teacher finds himself face to face with a question which involves one or the other of the three types given here. It is up to the teacher to know how to spot them and how to give a reply which corresponds to it.

PART THREE

METHODS AND TECHNIQUES

VII.

TEACHER-DIRECTED PRESENTATION AND DIALOGUE

THE teacher-directed presentation, followed by dialogue, is the most widely known and used approach in religious education today. The very expression itself indicates its characteristics, namely, an introduction, lecture, or talk by the teacher which is so organized that it provokes in the students a living reaction of thought and assimilation.

1. ITS USE IN RELIGIOUS EDUCATION

Applied in religious education, the value of this approach depends on the aims which the teacher has for his students. In this approach to giving a knowledge of the faith, any talk or lecture addressed only to the intelligence, presented as a ready-made solution to problems of the faith, would be unfaithful to good teaching and to Revelation itself.

1. *Requirements for and Education in the Faith*

We cannot speak of someone having a knowledge of the faith until that moment when the student recreates within himself what is offered to him; or, more exactly, when he lets himself be recreated by the Word of God. Since we are dealing with wisdom, more than with doctrine, it must be tasted.

The religion teacher, therefore, cannot consider himself simply as a teacher of religion. The ordinary norms of formal presentation in teaching are inadequate here. It is not enough to be clear, logical, and interesting. The Word of God must be assimilated and that requires an active involvement. The elements of faith, under pain of remaining outside the person, must be interiorized. Knowledge of the faith exists only to the extent that there is vital adherence to the Message of Christ.

The teacher, then, is to lead the students to react personally in dialogue and exchange, to reflect and assimilate in silence the Word which has been announced to them, to recreate the Word in action.

2. *Creative Action of the Word*

God reveals Himself and makes Himself known only in that instant when His Word recreates the heart of man. The nature of Revelation is to convert, to turn man about, to transform him, interiorly to illuminate his intelligence, to change his deepest motivations. The Spirit of the Lord penetrates to the very heart of man to create there a new way of being.

Did Christ reveal Himself in the Gospel—think of Zacchaeus, or the Samaritan woman—without effecting by this revelation a radical transformation at the heart of man?

We can see what a distance separates this knowledge of the faith from a purely notional or intellectual knowledge.

2. PROVOKING A MEANINGFUL RESPONSE

The teacher will be aware of the need for a continuing human contact, a living and affective relationship with the entire class.

This statement is not just a reminder of what has been stressed before; it is an essential element here. Without a climate of sympathy and mutual esteem, without a friendly relationship with the adolescents, and mutual esteem, without a friendly relationship with the adolescents, it will be impossible to provoke an active response on the part of the students. When the class is at odds with the teacher, it becomes necessary to relax the atmosphere, to reëstablish or establish bonds, to create relationships. Contacts outside of class, then, may be very important.

Thus the Confraternity teacher, who meets a class once a week, has a difficult obstacle that he must in some way overcome if he wants to effect an authentic catechesis.

The presentation must follow an inductive rather than deductive approach.

In religious education, the presentation of material has to be thought out in a special fashion. Experience has taught us that whoever opens with abstractions is bound to fail. We should examine here the two ways of proceding in presentation: from the abstract; and, then, from the concrete.

(1) *The abstract.* Abstractions are used by the intelligence in order to structure or analyze a doctrine. Its characteristic is that it is notional.

Certainly, a predominantly didactic approach to religious education does not ignore the relationship between the doctrinal revelation and the student called to understand it; but this is not its primary interest.

> Doctrine places itself on an objective level which makes, at least provisionally, abstraction from the relationships between the object known and the knowing object. Working with ideas, analyzing and synthesizing, it is most interested in the link which attaches one truth to another; it seeks to perceive the relationships which the different intelligible aspects of the mystery have among themselves, and it shows the internal order of the mystery. The logic of its procedure finds itself, thus, determined by the goal.[1]

With this approach the teacher could develop the doctrinal presentation on the Eucharist based on two ideas contained within it: the sacrament, the sacrifice.

(2) *The concrete.* This presentation, from the beginning, wishes to lead to an intimate knowledge, involving the person's reactions. What characterizes it is the relational aspect.

The primary aim here is not so much the knowledge of a truth as a lead or introduction into a relationship, into sympathy, and finally into affective communion of love expressed by God. What is known in this way is what is experienced.

[1] Marcel van Caster, "Sagesse et Doctrine en catéchèse," *Lumen Vitae,* no. 54, 1963, p. 662.

Here things other than notional connections come into play, for example, the vital relationships between the interests and openness of the student. The teacher will have to find the opening by which the Word of God, in a particular mystery, comes into contact with interests of the group. In this approach, then, he would present the Eucharist by starting from the common experience of the students.

In any case, he must ask himself: In what way does this part of Christ's Message affect the students' desires to live and act, their drives and hopes? The Message of the seeking God which comes to meet man is then presented as the Good News which exceeds all hopes.

The teacher, finally, must seek to determine how a particular aspect of Christ's Message has and can change man's life and how this insertion of a new element in man's life can be concretized in behavior and actions that express the mystery.

The teacher-directed presentation in religious education calls for the second approach, precisely because it requires a constant dialogue with the whole man. It is at this wider and existential level, and not purely at the notional or intellectual, that the teacher can reach his students. The adolescent's psychology, in which intelligence, heart, affectivity, and action are closely interwoven, demands that the Message deal with him wholly. The heart of the art of teaching here, then, consists in finding the basic approach for our religious education.

There are four points to be considered in our approach to the class:

(1) *The teacher is one with his class.* The first words, the gestures, must create a bond with the students. In order that the

adolescents find themselves in the Message of Christ which the teacher wants to announce to them, he must communicate in their thoughts and hopes, he must bind himself to them in a really common experience.

As an example, in a class on the providence of God he might open with a question such as this:

—At the age of 15, as at 20 or 40, we all think of the future. Are you sometimes disturbed about the future?

Students can sense that their personal problem is also the problem of the teacher, and together they will set out to encounter the truth. This is indeed an incarnational method.

(2) *The teacher questions and challenges the students' thinking.* It is not enough to be one with the students. The teacher is the one who helps them go beyond their own limitations. He can and should intervene, in the name of the faith, to question their too earthly manner of seeing things. He broaches the question of God's point of view.

Regarding God's providence, for example, the teacher could interrupt with this rather abrupt question: "You look ahead, you want to organize the future. . . . But where does God fit into it all?"

If it were a question of the presence of the Church in the world, the teacher might say to them: "Imagine that the Church does not exist."

In challenging or shocking, according to the abilities of the class and their background, the teacher is trying to dispute easy solutions and bring to birth the hope of a richer insight—that brought by the Word of God. Good questioning can shake false premises and give rise to real questions.

The whole area of teaching questions is rather difficult to

explore in so brief a space as this chapter. A challenge can be fruitful, but also destructive if the student stops at the challenge, not seeing beyond. Yet, if we do not help the student go beyond his own thinking, we are failing him. Experience and discretion are absolute requirements, with the latter a real help in the beginning.

(3) *The teacher announces the Word of God.* At the summit of a human problem, after having aroused a class and led them to search for an answer, the teacher announces or shares the Good News of Jesus Christ. Here the message of Christ must touch the students, not as a simple intellectual response to the problem posed, but as a new light which goes beyond man's question and sometimes changes it completely.

This is not a simple step. In some cases it may not be arrived at for some time, after many classes, if the students are not fully aware of the dimensions of a problem. At other times, the Word of God is imposed too lightly and quickly, and then rejected.

(4) *The teacher develops the relationship between the Word of God and the problem at hand.* After the Message of Christ has been announced there must be a development, an enlargement of the relationship between the students' questions and the Message of Christ, especially on the level of everyday existence.

Again, regarding God's providence, the teacher would develop some of the following ideas:

—The best realization of human existence is achieved by adhering to the Kingdom.

—Even in the matter of everyday existence, God takes care, in some way, of whoever commits himself to the Kingdom.

These four points are only sketched here in broad outline.

The opening of a human being to another demands sensitivity and technique, and the range of responses is infinite. The four points do not flow evenly one into the other; sometimes a teacher may not get beyond the second or third point for many reasons. The aim of the teacher is to reveal the fullness of Christ's Message. He must at least keep the points in mind and continue to aim at achieving them.

Student response must be stimulated.

Techniques are needed to stimulate student response from a class, to get and keep their attention, to stimulate research and thought so as to promote a growing adherence to the faith and an assimilation of the Word of God. Our Lord knew how to arouse and hold interest because He knew man. He did not proceed from abstractions but from the world around Him.

A. TECHNIQUES FOR BRINGING THE CLASS TO LIFE

Here it is a question of techniques which, used in religious education, help the students to discover experiences personally, to find ways of acting and attitudes that are directly related to the Good News. Techniques must be developed, which will remove religious education from the purely intellectual realm.

—*The use of visual aids* such as films, illustrations, and photographs can provoke a wide range of discussion and interest. Advertisements from magazines can be used to show various meanings given to happiness. Popular songs—for example, "The Sound of Silence"—are provocative for the meaning of life today. The students themselves can be brought to involve themselves in such materials.

—*The use of everyday expressions, current quotations, and slogans* can call forth a reaction. The student should begin to see relationships between the world he lives in and the world of faith he is approaching.

—*The teacher calls on one of the students to sum up what has been said.* When the class is approaching an important point, it is good to involve more directly one of the students who can sum up the main points. In addition to helping the students see the discussion through another's eyes, this technique forces the particular student to search out what is essential.

—*The use of the blackboard* can help the student learn with his whole body. Teachers sometimes forget that the appeal to the eye, the placing of key phrases and words where they can be seen and seen again, can be an invaluable aid.

—*The judicious use of testing* ought always to be carried out, especially testing in which the student can reveal himself or find out what others are thinking. Very often, students want to express themselves but are more relaxed in writing about their feelings than in speaking about them. For example, in a unit on friendship, the teacher might arouse interest by having the students write on the topic: how to make oneself hateful, or how to make oneself congenial.

The whole area of technique offers much in the way of experimentation. The first thing to be considered is the teacher himself and his own ability to relate to others. Some have a spontaneous way that easily sees what will bring life to another; others need to plan carefully and critically if they are to achieve the same end. This is not a question of fun and games that amuse and are dropped; more, it is the question of realizing that man opens to man more easily when he is met on common ground and when he is approached through consideration. To ignore the needs of another, in terms of language, interest, abilities, is to ignore the other. The teacher goes out to the student by reaching into his world, the world where he can be met, and in which he needs help.

B. STIMULATING REFLECTION AND ASSIMILATION OF THE MESSAGE OF CHRIST

Christ's Message must convert the young person in his being and thinking; it must penetrate into him and be "recreated" during a time of reflection and personal prayer. The teacher can help in this process by extending the ideas and reactions of the class outside the class time.

One approach that has proved successful has been the use of some type of notebook. From the catechetical point of view, the notebook can be the place where the student recreates, under the impulse of the Holy Spirit, the material discussed and explored in class. Depending on the students' ages, the teacher will more or less leave the initiative up to them in this matter.

How to make up notes?

(1) *Take down.* The student is invited to take down the discussion summary or résumé of material covered in class. The résumé will be brief, consisting of the key phrases and important words. The purpose is to give the student the necessary material for personal reflection.

(2) *Recreate.* To complete the résumé the student is asked to note his own thoughts and personal discovery. To do this, he

will be able to cite incidents and outside reading including the Scriptures, and then he should write down once more what he has understood and what questions he might ask.

Here the student is called to face what he thinks and what he lives with what he has just learned. This personal work allows a beginning assimilation of the Message of Christ which could change his life, his thoughts and actions. From this first assimilation, his experiences in liturgy and any apostolate will furnish greater depth.

Another way of taking notes, especially with CCD classes, might be in the form of brief essays in which the students try to think out what they have discovered, but now in their own terms. Some type of reflection here is necessary if we are to hope for some assimilation.

It also follows that some reflection will occur at any time and point in a student's day. A crisis in his life may call forth and integrate material that has remained on the surface, but which needed some stimulus before it could be absorbed.[2]

3. THE VALUE OF THE TEACHER-DIRECTED DIALOGUE

(1) *This approach works well with the intellectually oriented* who are accustomed to listening, dialoguing, and absorbing. For some students, an emphasis on research, for example, would throw them out of their element since they are more accustomed to teacher direction.

[2] Cf. *Options.*

(2) *It is good for adolescents in general:* At an age when thought is closely linked to experience, the presence of the teacher helps to make the connection more clearly and accurately; also, at an age of questioning and searching, the approach still allows a place for concrete position, and encourages interior assimilation.

(3) *It is good from the standpoint of religious education.* It envisions, in fact, it provokes with a maximum of force what St. Paul calls "the obedience of faith." How? In bringing together in the best way the two focal points of the act of faith which are to receive and to act. The active dialogue and disclosure of the Good News involves opening the student as well as calling him to reflect and react.

VIII.

GROUP STUDY AND DISCUSSION

1. THE BASIC CONCEPTS

By group study and discussion we mean an approach which involves the entire class in the discovery and understanding of a particular doctrine or topic. While it starts from questioning by the teacher, this approach aims at a collective search and discovery by the class itself, under the direction and guidance of the teacher.

More specifically:

(1) The explicit statement of some aspect of Christ's Message comes when each student shares with the others his own insights on a certain doctrine, aided by the necessary help from the teacher, especially in the concluding summary. This differs from the more direct teaching approach in which the teacher frequently presents the doctrinal statement and proceeds to explain; here it is arrived at more obliquely, perhaps, but more directly by the students.

(2) This active discovery on the part of the students requires adolescents who can reflect on their faith, possess some

minimum amount of religious knowledge, and are already in some way a part of the life of the Church. Study and discussion by students demand that each have something to share; they cannot go into class empty-handed and with nothing to give.

(3) This method is not just an attention-getting device used to arouse the interest of the students in order to proceed to the more formal teacher-directed approach. It is not a pre-catechesis aimed at arousing and creating an atmosphere favorable for a doctrinal teaching which follows after the students are ready. The method proposed here is meant as a vehicle for an authentic exploration in religious education.

2. THE PROCEDURE

The teacher presents a problem to the group clearly and in a few words; if necessary he explains ambiguous terms by examples or definition. The class is then divided into small discussion and study groups, seven or eight at the most, who seek an answer together.

1. *The Question or Problem for the Group*

A. WHAT QUESTIONS OR PROBLEMS SHOULD BE USED?

The teacher proposes a possibly controversial situation, a problem to be solved, or a direct question. The aim is to arouse interest, provoke discussion, bring the group together in study. In this he hopes to involve the total person of the student, heart, will, intelligence.

(1) While it may seem strange, it is impossible to ask a really good question if the teacher has not first defined the *exact response or answer* which is to be given. The reason is simple: the answer must be implicitly contained in the question. The teacher, then, must first of all think out what he is trying to have the students reach in this discussion. Teachers must thus be very careful to define their aims in precise terms.

(2) Also, the teacher must discover what area of doctrine under discussion will interest the students to the greatest extent. He must see clearly how some part of a particular doctrine affects their lives and thinking, to which experiences it is related, how it might change them.

(3) Perhaps it may at times be helpful to have some of the students prepare the question or the problem under the guidance of the teacher.

Nothing is more important or more delicate than posing true questions: upon the quality of the question depends the quality of the class. The ideal question to be asked of adolescents will be the one which establishes a link between the doctrine to be announced to them and their needs, their lives, and their experiences.

If a teacher has carefully considered and formulated the doctrinal and psychological foundations of his program, it should be relatively easy for him to find a question which expresses the interests of the students in relation to some particular topic.

Here, for example, is a typical question which could be asked on prayer: "Does man really reach God by prayer?" Seemingly impersonal, this question touches the vital interest of the group, namely, the recurring difficulties of man's needs and the difficulties of reaching God. Caught up in a personal situation, the students can find themselves with a problem in their own lives: their own needs and difficulties in praying, their own egocentric manner (which is here called to transformation) of praying without relying on Christ. At the end of the discussion, it is to be hoped, they will arrive at a reality of faith: it is through Jesus Christ that a person reaches God in prayer. The point of the Message that the teacher must therefore consider is that no prayer is really possible or effective outside of Jesus Christ. The question is thus determined by the previously thought-out doctrinal point and the answer wanted.

B. HOW TO PRESENT THE QUESTION OR PROBLEM

If time is limited (and this is a major problem in a CCD program), the question or problem must be strong, concrete, and concise. In these situations, perhaps only one question will be used. Sometimes, however, it might be necessary to use several in order to give direction to the group study and discussion. Everything will depend on the group and its practice in group study and discussion.

It is not advisable to confine oneself to verbal questions always. A picture, movie scene, newspaper clipping, a slogan or a poster might be equally effective in opening up the group.

The choice of one of the above must be carefully weighed since here, also, the answer must be contained in the problem presented. The image or example used must be very meaningful. There is also the difficulty in the case of a newspaper clipping or the like in getting a copy for each group to work from.

2. *Study and Discussion in the Small Group*

The heart of this approach is found in the liveliness in small group discussions. Each one in the group must involve himself in the group search: first taking his own position, but then remaining attentive to the thinking of the others. Each student must respect and listen to the others, for exchange and discussion involves both openness and attentiveness.

It is very important to make clear that the goal of the small group is not to argue the different points of view. That is for the general discussion. The objective in the small groupings is to permit everyone to express himself, to give his point of view. The range of opinions gathered in the groups will provide the basis for the class discussion.

Each small group chooses for itself a leader and a secretary. The task of the leader will be to stimulate open answers, the positions which each one will later have to defend. He should know how to put each one at ease and get him to express himself. He might ask: "What is your answer?" He can, if the occasion presents itself, show how one answer differs from another. If necessary, he should ask for a clarification or an example.

In the course of this dialogue, the secretary takes notes to be used with the general discussion.

3. *Exchange and Discussion With the Entire Group*

The smaller groups come together for a general discussion led by the teacher. (The arrangement of the room should permit good hearing and viewing of all the students.) The purpose is to present different points of view which must be defended, deepened, or possibly dropped. Each student is put in the position of listening, and then trying to understand and seek the truth contained in each position.

A. PRESENTING OPINIONS

The secretary of the first group gives an account of the work of his group. The teacher will ask for clarifications: "Is this really the thought of each member of the group? Do you have any examples?" He will then ask the entire class, "Have you any questions?", making sure that each person in the entire group has fully understood the first report.

Passing then to the second group, he will ask the secretary not to repeat what may have already been said, but to give only those points of view which were not given by the first group. The teacher can also repeat what has been said in different words and ask for the agreement of the second group: "Is this what you really intended to say?" This procedure if followed for each group.

B. DISCUSSION

As the reports progress, the teacher will note the comments, discoveries, and elements of the answer which seem essential to him. A good procedure would be to write on the blackboard, if possible, the major lines of the answers as they emerge from the reports. He will, if necessary, clarify any obscure points which could create problems.

His objective, now, is to get the group to discuss the basic problems. The differing points of view must be defended, rethought, reëvaluated. The role of the teacher is as follows:

(1) He keeps the discussion moving, raising questions, comparing, praising, and often throwing a hard light on a contribution of one of the small groups; he draws out the whole meaning of some insight or answer.

(2) He approves one after the other the elements of truth as they emerge, putting the whole weight of his authority into the approval of what has been said, or possibly emphasizing the group's disapproval of a point.

(3) He contributes new material as needed, proposes new lines of thought, especially when the group has not sufficiently explained a doctrinal point.

(4) He concludes the discussion with a clear and precise formulation or summary.

C. CONCLUSION

At the end of the discussion, the teacher will present a synthesis (or perhaps help the students to do it themselves) of the points presented for discussion. He takes up the ideas given by the group in order to shape it into a conclusion which brings order and security to their minds. The answer is stated in a clear, precise, and, if possible, structured formula or statement.

Sometimes the teacher will go back to a particular expression of some student in order to comment on it in a meditative way, relate it to biblical texts, and thus introduce a kind of silent prayer.

3. RULES FOR GROUP DISCUSSION

Group discussion is not improvised: it demands that the teacher, in order to be effective in the matter of faith and discussion, have assured competence, mastery of self, skill in discussion, and a long training with groups. It demands a real discipline of dialogue on the part of the students so that *each one expresses himself for all and that all express themselves for each.*

The rules proposed here express at once spiritual and practical demands. It would be good to explain them to the students and gradually to impose them with authority. These are not simply procedures; they are first of all the behavior of charity.

(1) Before discussing an opinion or taking a position, obtain from the one who gave it the maximum of precision and clarification in a climate of great objectivity.

(2) When someone has the floor, it is forbidden to interrupt; wait until he is finished before questioning him.

(3) Before asking a question, ask yourself if it will interest the whole group. If it is a matter which interests only a minority, keep silent. When a student keeps asking questions that are off the subject, the leader will try to correct him either by letting the question drop or by asking him to explain himself alone after the discussion.

(4) It is forbidden to think out loud. Before speaking, each one should carefully outline his position.

(5) When the discussion does not go forward or when it becomes lost in generalities, start asking for facts and concrete examples.

4. USING GROUP DISCUSSION WITH ADOLESCENTS

Group study and discussion, difficult to realize with adolescents, is one of the key methods for religious education. If it cannot be used on a regular basis, it should at least be used from time to time for reducing the tension of a highly structured class, for awakening and encouraging the curiosity of the students, and for bringing them together with one another and the teacher.

Problems in using group discussion vary from one age group to another. With the thirteen to fifteen year olds, accustomed to a more formal approach, the difficulty springs from the instability and egocentricity which characterizes that age, and inhibits or hurts the discussion. If a group is not too large, the teacher can use the method occasionally and with some variations, especially with an eye to a progressive education in the method.

With those from sixteen to eighteen who are accustomed to the individualistic student-teacher relation and are used to a regime of systematic teaching, the teacher will have difficulty in setting up a real dialogue and getting under way a true search for truth with a group.

He should go slowly and take care to handle topics that can be summarized more easily so that the student will feel himself at ease and have the impression of having learned something.

For some students, however, this approach can work regularly. It is well adapted to the manner of living and working today; more, it stresses the involvement of the group in thinking and action. It invites them to dialogue and the meeting of others which will occur in adult life.

5. VALUES FOR RELIGIOUS EDUCATION

The discovery of truth in this approach is brought about:

—*by the involvement of each student* in taking a position which he must understand and defend in the face of others;

—*by the deepening of the discussion* led by the teacher who pushes the questions to their limits, that is, getting at all of the implications;

—*by the final intervention of the teacher* who formulates the doctrine in a clear and precise way.

No doubt, this is a difficult method to use effectively. It demands much practice and a patient formation of the students. But it can be much more effective than the traditional form of teaching for educating the adolescents to the life of faith and charity.

(1) It educates them to the faith. Teaching them to listen is, after all, making them attentive to Jesus Christ. It opens them; it disposes them for the signs of the faith.

(2) It educates them to charity. Teaching them to dialogue is teaching them to communicate with one another in the charity of Jesus Christ. Teaching them to advance in discussion is teaching them the design of the Holy Spirit who moves forward with men, who builds, who works in love, who effectively builds the community.

It may be said that such a method well applied builds the Church.

IX.

READING AND RESEARCH

1. REQUIRED READINGS

THE method of required reading was used very much by the communists in study circles. Douglas Hyde has written: "The group was given the required reading. This was reduced to a minimum: a few pages of a book, for example, or a chapter in another. The students who once missed a reading were not slow in seeing that they must do it in the future under pain of not understanding the lesson and of seeing their negligence come out before their comrades in the course of the discussion."[1]

This is a perennial problem in the field of religious education. While it may be more strongly felt in a CCD situation, it sometimes presents difficulties in the everyday classroom situation as well. Sanctions, of course, are used by some teachers, but that raises issues which fall outside of the scope of this work. It should be said, however, that the problem of assignments and sanctions as the teacher attempts to create an atmosphere of openness and acceptance is a very difficult one to solve in light of the many and various needs and interests of the entire class. Part of the problem may be in the teacher himself, who mistakenly judges the stu-

[1] Cited in *Le Christ au monde,* no. 6.

dents' displeasure over assignments to be more serious than it actually is. Students not infrequently dislike assignments. An atmosphere of openness and freedom is not created by giving the students *carte blanche,* but by helping them to grow by knowing, exploring, thinking. The role of the teacher is to guide and also to lead.

One thing to examine carefully is the material given for reading. Much material is excellent and once the students are reading, there is little problem. Other material, perhaps, should be closely examined. Teachers should occasionally view material in terms of students' interests and abilities. Encyclicals, for instance, can at times be very difficult reading.

Just as critical is what is done with the material read. If the assignment is given for such and such a date, every effort should be made to use it then. Simple pedagogical common sense is a great help there.

An assignment in reading takes on new meaning when questions are given which help to direct the thinking of the reader. A road map is valuable and interesting only when there is something to look for; one then has a broad view of an area in relation to a specific need. A student does not always bring something of his own to what he reads; he frequently needs something to look for, something on which to focus his attention in order that his reading may be purposeful.

What should be done if the students do not read, or have not read enough to get involved in a class discussion? The teacher has no ready answer for that until he knows his group, his own relationship to them, their reasons for not reading, and even their level of faith. In some CCD situations it is almost impossible to be sure of home assignments; some assignments may have to be done on class time. Sometimes the group can urge remiss students to catch up in their assignments. Occasionally, in a graded situation, brief quizzes can help, although the teacher must think out his own approach to tests and sanctions. Testing is very good with many students since they realize that they need to be prodded into reading and reporting. An honest exchange with the students on this problem is probably the quickest and best way to solve it.

2. RESEARCH

Another aid for students is the exploration and preparation of material on some topic which the teacher and group want to cover.

Several things must be done:

(1) After a decision has been reached on a subject, the teacher assigns or takes volunteers to prepare material for the class by a given date.

(2) The teacher should furnish some leads for the students—for example, what material is available and helpful, which people might be interviewed as resource persons.

(3) Some division of labor is worked out, preferably under guidance of the teacher, when a group is doing this work.

It is to be hoped that the teacher will be available to the students for advice, suggesting ideas, giving criticisms, guiding their research, and helping them prepare for the actual presentation.

This method can be extremely helpful to a student, a group, the class; but it also has some drawbacks that must be considered. Few things are duller or more apt to create discipline problems than a poor presentation of material by students not really prepared for it. Many teachers know how restless the teacher and students can be when oral book reports are given.

On the other hand, a well-prepared presentation gives it a sense of urgency because it is given by the students; and for the students involved, it has been something they have discovered on their own and are eager to share with others.

X.

THE INTERVIEW

1. THE VALUE OF INTERVIEW FOR THE RELIGIOUS EDUCATION OF ADOLESCENTS

THE interview offers a special value for our times. Its use on television and in newspapers attests to this fact, for the interview responds to modern man's sensitive need to know what other men are saying and also to see his own thoughts in relation to those of others.

1. *Awareness of Others' Opinions*

Considered in terms of religious education, the interview helps the students become actively aware of the personal or collective opinions of their contemporaries on a given subject. The students can then see their Christian viewpoint more realistically in the context of the world around them. Tomorrow, the adolescents will be living in a world where it will no longer be tradition which serves as the model and norm of behavior as in the past, but opinion. Hence we must stress the importance of their becoming aware of this sociological factor.

For the present, it is necessary that they train themselves in discovering tendencies and collective currents, passing them through the crucible of criticism, and then also learning to stand back and judge with objectivity what people say and write. This effort seems to be indispensable if they are to grow to the true freedom of the children of God.

2. *Dialogue With Others*

Through the interview, adolescents are led to enter into dialogue with others. They have to ask questions, to take seriously those with whom they speak, hear them with sympathy and respect, represent themselves honestly before men who may not think as they do. This attitude of openness and understanding can help them to surmount the egocentrism of their years; it is an apprenticeship in dialogue, which strengthens their own personalities, and is also an education in true charity.

3. *Direct Participation in Their Religious Education*

By means of the interview, the students take an active part in preparation for the class meetings. This stimulating activity, thanks to contact outside the class, keeps them from the passivity of ready-made positions and can give them an appetite for the deepening of their knowledge of the faith.

2. THE USE OF THE INTERVIEW IN RELIGIOUS EDUCATION

The teacher can use the interview either as a starting point or as a teaching technique.

1. *Starting Point*

A. FOR A DIALOGUE WITH THE TEACHER

For example, after conducting an inquiry into what people think about happiness, the students present the results in common. In a certain way, this expression of collective opinion, which may challenge the students' opinions, helps the teacher to form a bond with his students, to enter into their problems. With this step he can join the students in a true search for the meaning of happiness.

B. FOR A GROUP DISCUSSION

As in the first case, the students have conducted a survey on the meaning of happiness and have presented it in common. Now they have to go further and discuss it and make a judgment for themselves on what they have surveyed. The interview was a starter, making them sensitive to the problem. It opened them to the Message of Jesus Christ. Now the students form into small groups in order to explore the profounder aspects of happiness. They could perhaps begin by answering a question asked by the teacher, such as "What is happiness for you?"

A presentation in common, according to the group-discussion method, will permit the students to list the components of happiness (the joys of creative work, the discovery of friendship, of love . . .). Without too much difficulty, the group may eventually reach the definite question: "What kind of happiness has God willed for us?"

2. *The Interview Used in the Teaching Situation*

Such an interview could be had, for example, with a contemplative religious. From this dialogue, the teacher could pick out the diverse characteristics of the vocation to build his talk and to illustrate it. Here he gathers together the elements of a catechesis already contained in the interview; he emphasizes them and structures them.

3. PREPARING THE INTERVIEW

1. *Who Is to Be Interviewed?*

(1) *The class itself.* Interviews could be done with members of the class, and using these results as a base, an effective program could be formulated whose aim is to clear up judgments and offer answers to objections which came out of the interviews.

For example, two students could be put in charge of getting the opinion of the class on the following subject: "What do you think about the history of the Church? What does it contribute to your life as a Christian?"

The class interview has two advantages:

—the teacher discovers what the class is thinking;

—the group is brought together by collective reflection and research.

(2) *A person involved in special work or in a typical profession.* This type of personal opinion or testimony will be individual and quite personal. In this way the students may meet a union leader,

a poverty-program worker, perhaps a cloistered religious, and then question him on his life, the meaning of his involvement with others, his vocation or profession.

The fact that the students question persons who are at once competent and also involved in life has a double advantage: that of answers which are enriching for the interview purposes, and also, and as important, that of contacts with adults in a climate favoring dialogue and understanding.

(3) *Persons different from the students in terms of background, age, profession.* "Are you happy? What makes you happy?" These are the questions that students could ask of random strangers, possibly reaching a large number of persons who would give their spontaneous answers. This sampling will not, of course, be complete; but the implications gathered will nevertheless help the students pick out the different currents of opinion.

This kind of interview may not prove practical in many areas or with many students. Another aspect of such an interview would be to involve students with people of different social, economic, and cultural backgrounds. This is rather difficult unless some meeting of equality is achieved between the differing groups. In any case, the teacher must be careful to guide the students in a sense of charity and tact.

2. *What Questions Should be Asked?*

The choice and the formulation of questions are of critical importance. If a question is to evoke an answer, it must be posed in such a way that it is not ambiguous and that it tells the person interviewed exactly what is expected of him.

(1) Before stating a question, the student should define its objective, draw up a list of what he wants to know, and anticipate the direction which the questioning should develop.

If the student is interviewing someone on the question of work, he should decide what part of the topic he wants to ask about: for example, work and family life, relationships with other workers, fulfillment in work, and so forth. In the last case, he could ask the following: "What do you think of your work? Are you happy in your work?"

(2) After the student has decided on the basic approach, the teacher should help him to formulate the actual questions from the lead one to possible follow-up areas.

(3) The student should phrase his questions in a personal way, since he is asking for personal testimony: "What do *you* think . . . ?"

3. *The Interview Itself*

Prepared with precise questions, two students should go on the interview. The students should make it known that, if the interviewee agrees, one student will ask the questions while the other takes notes. In that way the one interviewing will be able to concentrate totally on the interview. The one taking notes should take them on the spot, if that also has been agreed upon. Otherwise, the comments should be noted down as soon afterwards as possible. Another possibility is the use of a tape recorder. A tape is a faithful reproduction of the interview, and it can perhaps be played for the whole class, who will then, in a way, be able to relive the interview.

4. THE USE OF THE INTERVIEW IN CLASS

Once the information from the interview has been obtained, the teacher will help the student interviewers assemble, classify, judge, and prepare the material for presentation.

(1) If many students are involved in the interview, they should bring together all of the material obtained.

(2) They should then classify the diverse thoughts expressed in the interviews and if necessary compare them through a statistical method. Afterwards, they should attempt a synthesis of all the diverse opinions.

In the case of a single interview which is rather important and full, it will also be necessary to structure and order the different parts of the interview.

(3) The students will have to be involved in some type of judgment. Judgment demands that:

—they interpret the results of their interviews. "In our opinion, it seems to us that if people say this, it may mean that . . .";

—they set up a kind of comparison of the results with moral and doctrinal norms;

—they make, if possible, a personal value judgment: "We agree (or we do not agree) because . . ."

(4) They present the results to the group. This presentation involves the same difficulties and possibilities that the presentation of outside reading involves.

XI.

STUDENT PRESENTATIONS: THE PANEL, ROLE-PLAYING, THE TRIBUNAL

THE methods already presented and analyzed were designed to help the students grow in research directed to clarifying particular points of doctrine. The three in this chapter, the panel, role-playing, and the tribunal, have as their objective the taking of positions by the group faced with the Christian Message, and the deepening and assimilating of the Good News within their own lives.

1. THE PANEL

1. *The Basic Concept*

The panel is a forum of exchange before a group, large or small, in which several students present their points of view on a given subject, giving the basis for their particular stand. Since each student on a panel should represent a different view (but one that is valid), the positions taken should give rise to questions and foster a discussion between the members of the panel and the audience.

Required elements:

(1) The subject for presentation should allow of different but valid approaches.

(2) The members of the panel should be committed to the approach which they themselves present.

(3) The members of the audience must have the right and the time to question the panel.

As used specifically in religious education, the panel should not just be a simple confrontation of opinions, but should be a way of announcing the Message of Christ.

2. *The Aim of the Panel in Religious Education*

The panel has as its aim the involvement of the students in some aspect of the Christian Message, and then help them understand and enrich their thoughts on that topic.

A. TO THINK OUT THE APPROACHES AND REASONS FOR DIFFERING VIEWPOINTS

Each panel discussion may include students who, sharing the same fundamental perspectives of faith and finding themselves before the same problem in life, have come up with different points of view. The goal of the panel is to find out how each of the choices can be legitimately related to the same faith; then the strong points of each approach should be discussed and analyzed.

The panel has the great advantage of making each participant and observer understand the other, his way of thinking and acting. Also, it forces a student to reëvaluate his own thinking and motivation in a particular area. If a student comes to the panel with the idea of pushing his points across instead of presenting an approach, he may run the risk of not listening to his companions and of not welcoming the ideas of the other panel members. He may also be discouraged if his own ideas do not prevail.

A panel encourages each member to discover where his thinking fits into the Church, in the face of other valid opinions. This can be the first introduction into the adult involvement which, hopefully, will have to be neither totalitarian nor sectarian, but complementary to others. Finally, the panel promotes a respect for others which helps develop a more profound living of the life of the Church.

B. TO SHOW THE DOCTRINAL MESSAGE IN CONJUNCTION WITH THE POSSIBLE APPROACHES

Another goal of the panel is to underline the Message of Christ that is contained in the different viewpoints. In this approach Christ's truth is seen to be not some theory detached from life and all commitment.

In actuality, the panel is not meant to affect doctrinal reality, because for the Christian the data of faith are not debatable; one has not made a choice for or against the Word of God. Thus, for example, one could not have a panel on the two following propositions:

—faith is to commit oneself to the person of Christ;
—faith is to hold as true the doctrine of Christ.

A panel, then, is workable each time there is freedom of choice or opinion. Thus theologians can have discussion on predestination or prevenient grace: on these points, the definitions of the Church allow different choices. The choices, however, are more on the level of thought than of behavior.

In religious education, however, the panel must have an existential character. The teacher should not organize the panel merely for the pleasure of a meeting of opinions. Each participant must present and defend a choice of faith which always has its origins in some kind of conversion and which expresses itself in the concrete taking of sides leading to action. What a student is led to explain in a panel is the "why" of his actions, the source of his motivation.

In a panel on the meaning of Mass and communion, where the student has begun to rethink and rediscover the vital question of sacramental practice, the Message of Christ will appear in connection with everyday existence.

3. *The Conditions Required For a Panel in Religious Education*

A. A SUBJECT WHICH INVOLVES DIFFERING BUT EQUALLY VALID CHOICES

The panel must be concerned wtih a subject that provides different but equally valid choices. The solution should not be given in advance, nor should the discussion be resolved before it has ever begun. That is why the panel does not have as its aim the vindication of any particular choice.

For example: A student is witness to a serious offense: the theft of exam questions by one of his friends With whom should he consult first, the authorities or his friend? Why?

B. PANEL MEMBERS SHOULD BE PERSONALLY INVOLVED IN THE POSITIONS THEY TAKE

Each participant should present and defend a choice to which he is really committed and to which he has given considerable reflection. A panel discussion is not a debate in the strict sense of the term. It would be difficult for a student with no work experience to defend the position that factory work brutalizes man and is contrary to his nature. The student is not forbidden to have his ideas on the subject; but not being a worker, he cannot validly take part in a panel.

N.B. To fulfill the requirement of real involvement in dealing with certain subjects such as marriage and work, the teacher should try to get adults who are themselves involved in these concrete situations to form a panel for which the class will be an audience.

C. AN AUDIENCE WHICH PARTICIPATES AND INVOLVES ITSELF

A panel is always situated in front of an audience which in some way takes part in the discussion. Its participation will be expressed in the form of questions which oblige the panel members to clarify and define their positions and perhaps even to rethink them in the face of objections raised by the group.

Finally, if the panel has sufficiently developed the topic, the audience will be made sensitive to the values involved and led to make a choice for one or other of the positions.

4. *The Preparation and Organization of a Panel*

A. THE SELECTION OF MEMBERS

The teacher will ask for volunteers or will himself choose the participants some time (two or three weeks) in advance of the scheduled date so as to allow sufficient preparation. He will explain to them the nature of a panel, its aim, procedure, and what is expected of them.

B. THE PREPARATION OF PANEL MEMBERS

Each participant must give considerable personal thought to the position he is going to defend. He should consult his friends, parents, teachers. He should be sure that he properly understands the doctrine that his viewpoint is related to. He must be ready to defend his position by clarifying it with facts and concrete examples. The use of examples will also help the other participants to understand his view. The quality of preparation determines the quality of the panel.

C. THE NUMBER AND ARRANGEMENT OF PANEL MEMBERS

The number of members can vary from four to ten; six or eight is the ideal, a group large enough for variety, small enough for a true dialogue. The students should be seated facing the audience, with the moderator in the center. The teacher should try to place the more timid next to the moderator so that he can easily question them.

D. THE ROLE OF THE MODERATOR

The moderator can be a member of the class, the teacher himself, or, to ensure impartiality or to free the teacher for observation, someone from outside.

The moderator will see to it that each person expresses himself without, however, following too definite an order. An authentic conversation is always spontaneous.

If the group has not been trained in exchange and discussion, the moderator's role can become more important and will be taken by the teacher preferably. He must then ask questions of each one and summarize the answers: "Is this what you want to say? Could you give an example?" He will direct the discussion and keep it moving; he will direct it towards new points of view when it bogs down. Above all, he will see to it that no one gets off the point and that the discussion arrives at its full development within the allotted time.

E. THE DIVISION OF TIME

5 minutes: presentation of the subject by the moderator.

20–40 minutes (according to the number on the panel): discussion among the panel members.

10–15 minutes: questions and discussions by audience directed to members of the panel.

5–10 minutes: conclusion by the moderator.

F. DISCUSSION DEVELOPMENT

(1) The moderator clearly presents the subjects and introduces the panel members.

(2) The panel members first dialogue among themselves in front of the audience. Each one expresses himself, presents his position, attacks that of another, or defends his own. It is essential that each position be clearly stated at the beginning so that everyone will know what the discussion is about.

The discussion needs a true climate of dialogue made up of sympathy, understanding, a powerful demand for truth, mutual respect, and friendship. To obtain this climate the moderator must truly moderate, and see that each student gets a chance to speak and that no one slows the progress of the discussion with needless digressions.

(3) The moderator will open the discussion to the audience at the scheduled time. If the discussion has been well directed, the audience will be interested and ask valid questions of the panel. The moderator should also allow relevant questions concerning points not raised in the panel discussion or issues which were only obscurely brought out; he should also, of course, allow members of the audience to voice valid objections.

G. CLARIFICATION AND UNDERSTANDING OF DOCTRINAL POINTS DISCUSSED

As much as possible, each panel member should explain and defend the doctrinal basis of his position. If this is not feasible, then the teacher should give an explanation of the doctrine, starting from the discussion points made.

Finally, the moderator concludes the panel: on the one hand by clearly recapitulating the different points of view expressed, their validity, their limits; on the other hand by pointing out the doctrinal points which underlie the different positions. From these he can bring the class to see what has been expressed in the light of faith.

Panel discussions have played a role in television for many years and there have been some excellent panels directed to youth. A teacher should observe them and also ask his students to watch them, if possible, before the panel is used in class.

2. ROLE-PLAYING

Used in religious education, role-playing[1] is a method which consists in provoking a debate on a topic from a dramatization of a real-life situation which poses a problem for the class.

[1] We have not used here the term socio-drama, reserved for group psychotherapy. "The socio-drama," writes Guy Palmade, "is a technique which permits the exploration of the true image of social evils in a group, that is to say, the affective truth, often camouflaged beneath the real social structure and beneath the conflicts which it provokes, indicating the direction of desirable transformations through the medium of dramatic methods." *La Psychothérapie,* P. U. F., pp. 106–108.

We are using here a method used in the United States for the education of the young, a method which, however, has different forms. The National Conference of Christians and Jews has published an interesting pamphlet, with a bibliography, in this field. The pamphlet costs 25¢ and is entitled "Role Playing the Problem Story, an Approach to Human Relations in the Classroom," by George and Fannie R. Shaftel.

An approach with elementary school pupils that could provide insights in this

1. *Material to be Used*

Role playing must present a current life situation.

A. FIRST TYPE

The subject matter must always be taken from a context with which the class is familiar. It can simply present a problem, a situation in which persons are at odds with one another.

The first type is fairly uncomplicated. Here it is a question of asking certain students to reproduce before the group a scene of conflict, misunderstanding, or discord which is familiar to them because they have experienced it, or because they have observed it. Not demanding much in the way of original improvisation or effort of imagination, this form of a dramatic game is more for a group which is not yet accustomed to spontaneous self-expression. Some students are more willing to reproduce an anonymous scene, one not related to themselves, than to commit themselves personally. In this type of role-playing the student is obliged to improvise solutions and express personal positions.

B. SECOND TYPE

Here a scene is played out in which the students try to remedy an already existing wrong. In this case, the students are called upon to propose different ways of resolving the problem. This

---

area is the work of Joan Haggerty entitled *Please Can I Play God?* (New York, 1967). It is the story of an American woman teaching in an English school who uses this technique for literature.

form of role-playing is more difficult and presupposes a deeper knowledge of the faith.

Because it demands a response in which the person expresses a view and offers a solution, this type of role-playing leads the students to involve themselves in a more personal way in the scene they are playing, but it may also lead them to finding real solutions.

2. *The Basic Approach*

The scene should be kept simple, relatively serious, with a minimum of direction. The basic idea is an improvisation and not a minutely prepared script. The improvisation is valuable in that it can permit the students to express their true attitudes spontaneously. In most cases, players should be few, but enough to provide a representative range of opinion. Perhaps five to eight would be a guide.

3. *Conducting a Role-Playing Situation*

A. PRESENTING THE THEME

The teacher will, first of all, explain the procedures of role-playing to the class, opening them to its value while stressing the need for truth. The students should have a good understanding of the techniques and also the subject to be explored.

The teacher then presents the dramatic situation to be done—for example, the violation of a trust between friends, a conflict between parents and children. He sets the scene, describes the characters, and explains the conflict which is going to arise or which already exists. Then he may ask for volunteers to play the characters in the scene and to show their specific reactions in the face of this given situation.

(At times it may be advisable to be selective in the question of some volunteers. A student emotionally disturbed over his own relations to his parents would not be a suitable choice for a role in a parent-child situation. Role-playing in catechetics is not meant to be therapeutic and a teacher should be wary of unleashing an emotional situation before the class. Role-playing here is to arrive at a moral solution; this requires a certain stability, according to the age of the students. Knowledge of each student in the class is essential for this technique. Role-playing as a method for releasing tensions is one thing; but as used in the religious education of adolescents it is something quite different. Both demand skill; and, although they have somewhat similar approaches, their aims are different and demand great care so that unnecessary damage is avoided.)

B. THE SCENE ITSELF

The volunteers play the scene following the basic directions of the teacher. This should be a spontaneous affair in which the students freely express themselves. The scene should not go beyond five or ten minutes.

C. DISCUSSION

The teacher must get the class to discuss the religious meaning underlying the theme of the short presentation.

—The class, with the help of the teacher, analyzes the elements of the situation, the ideas expressed, the positions taken, and so forth.

—Then each student reacts to the interpretation given: "As for me, I would have done something else . . ."

—Finally, the teacher should ask: "Why did the play go this way? What did they wish to say? Why would you have acted otherwise . . . ?"

By his questions and direction, the teacher focusses the discussion and helps the class progressively head to an understanding of the faith answer which clarifies the situation and gives the key to the problem.

D. REPEATING THE SITUATION

The teacher then proposes that another group of volunteers play the same scene, who will take into account the clarifications contributed by the discussion.

If the teacher has directed the discussion well, if the class has reacted, then the repetition of the scene will incarnate the solutions and crystallize in the students' minds the different elements and new thoughts which were brought out in common.

4. *The Value of Role-Playing*

Role-playing is a catechetical method which places the students closer to real life and concrete realities. An apt method in terms of questions relating to the adolescents' moral life, it permits an interesting actualization of problems which might very well remain abstract. To speak of role-playing is to speak of spontaneity, invention, dramatic improvisation. The play becomes an instrument of work for the group, a means of self-expression, of self-education, and sometimes even of testimony to their faith.

Through the discussion provoked, role-playing stimulates the group to think out situations, compelling adolescents to a personal solution of a problem, asking them to find valid responses to conflict situations. In some cases, it may be a help to conquering timidity in the face of a group situation.

Finally, like the panel, role-playing permits the discovery and appearance of the doctrinal realities implicit in every position taken. This demands competence on the part of the teacher in stimulating and directing the class thinking, helping the students turn to doctrinal realities and not permitting the discussion to get away from him. In this way the students may be led to discover that nothing in their lives can be separated from their faith and from their own religious attitudes.

5. *An Example of Role-Playing on the Parent-Child Relationship*

A. THE CATECHETICAL AIM UNDERLYING THIS EXAMPLE

This role-playing situation is designed to show how the lack of understanding between parents and children can give rise to feelings of frustration and revolt and can, at worst, result in an emotional explosion within the family. Hence the importance of a relationship of true love between parents and children.

B. AN ACTUAL SCENE

a. An adolescent girl tries to explain to her parents a problem she has, but she does it in a clumsy way. She speaks to them about outings with her friends which she cannot go on because they are too expensive. Brusquely her father interrupts: "Say exactly what you mean. Perhaps your allowance isn't enough. It's easy to see you don't know what it means to earn a living! At your age . . ." The girl withdraws in silence.

b. Parents who do not understand the supposed aggressiveness of the daughter are ready, however, to do everything possible for her, and would like to help her. How?

C. DISCUSSION

Here are some of the questions and parts of the answers used in the discussion.

(1) What did the role-playing want to show?

The connection between the different scenes brought out a lack of understanding in which each side rejects the other in a type of silence and creates two camps. The conflict makes the parents unhappy and frustrates the girl emotionally.

The parents do not know how to give the girl the freedom for expression. They do not really listen to her. Everything is decided and resolved in advance with no reference to her.

The girl, caught up in her own personal problems, goes to the extent of saying that she "hates" her parents. "At no price will I give up."

(2) Did the acting out of the conflict solve anything?

The conflict did nothing but widen the gulf between the parents and the daughter.

(3) What is regrettable in this on-going conflict?

On the part of the parents: they will not accept the fact that their daughter is no longer a child, and they refuse to give her that minimum of choice which would permit her to develop a personal behavior. Why this attitude on their part?

On the part of the girl: she gives in to hate, violence, and pride. Why?

(4) How can this conflict be resolved?

The role of the teacher here is not so much that of one who expounds moral principles as that of asking questions capable of directing the students towards a true solution. For this particular situation, here are some typical questions:

(*a*) Has this girl reflected on what God expects of her, of what He thinks of this conflict? More exactly, has she perhaps brought about this break with her parents because of an infantile way of behaving with them? If she acts like a child, how are they going to treat her like an adult?

If she sees what God wants from her, is she prepared to behave more like an adult, with more reflection, even if her parents are not ready to consider her as such, and still continue to maintain their control over her freedom?

(*b*) Does this girl really love her parents?

Concretely, is she ready to pardon the hurtful words, to understand her parents, and to make them happy by some signs of attentiveness? Does she think of asking Christ for light and help?

(*c*) If the difficulties recur, should not this girl confide in a counselor who is at once understanding and honest with her?

D. REPEATING THE SCENE

Some volunteers repeat the scene from the moment when the conflict breaks out and try to express a solution more in conformity with Christian solutions.

3. THE TRIBUNAL

1. *The Basic Concept*

Borrowed from the world of justice, this method has as its aim to help the students inform themselves on some topic in a way that is active, lively, even combative, and gets them to take a side after some reflection.

This involves the expression and confrontation of different but valid points of view. The tribunal session permits a deepening of some questions raised by the students by making them seek human and religious justifications. An attractive technique, it works particularly well with boys of second- or third-year high school.

2. *Preparation*

For an example of this technique, a trial on the topic "Does the press always tell the truth?" will be used.

A. THE MATERIAL

The teacher or students should obtain copies of two politically opposed newspapers for one or two weeks. Articles should be selected that treat of the same subject but which are handled from different or even contrary perspectives.

The trial will be that of two newspapers accused of propaganda, of lying, and so on. Each will be defended by a lawyer and attacked by a prosecutor.

For adolescents not accustomed to dialogue, the teacher should avoid articles too controversial, such as political nominations, or strikes. Topics for this approach could include news items, books, or film reviews (does such and such a film present an authentic and valuable presentation of some problem).

What should be noted is that this technique can be helpful in opening students to forming views or obtaining information that is needed to function in our society, such as: In the question of the press there is contained the problem of a Christian conscience and its formation. Its use depends greatly on the area to be covered. In race relations, for example, this approach might be difficult if it puts a defendant on the spot and causes embarrassment. Basically, this is not a technique for personal indictment; rather, it is a way of exploring two sides of a topic and understanding them more fully.

B. THE SETTING

Arrange the room like a court-room: at the back, the public; in front, the witness stand (a small table); on the one side, two chairs for the defending lawyers; on the other, two for the prosecutors; finally, a table for the judge and some space for the jury.

Judge and lawyers can be chosen from the class leaders. The jury can be selected from the remainder of the class. Note, of course, that humor can arise from this type of session, but it should not detract from the seriousness of the topic.

3. *The Actual Trial*

(1) Entry of the court. All stand.

(2) Introduction of the case by the judge; a few words on the problem of information in our present society. Technical terms are given and explained.

From the beginning the class must see the difficulty in being well informed and in giving a valid judgment. That is why everyone, and particularly the Christian, must learn to inform himself so as to understand what is happening in his country and thus act intelligently in seeking such information. The judging of the press contains also a form of witness: Christians must oppose, in the commitment of their lives, all lying and hatred in any form.

(3) The indictment is read by the prosecutor.

(4) Time is allowed for everyone to study the evidence. The class is divided into several groups. Each group examines the newspaper articles chosen; each person who testifies chooses an article on which he will give his opinion. The defense lawyers will try to defend the material printed in the newspapers; the prosecution will attempt to provide criticism.

(5) The witnesses, those representing the papers, will be examined by the defense and the prosecution.

(6) After the witnesses there will be a time for summations by the prosecutor and the defense.

(7) The court retires to deliberate; the verdict and then sentencing, if necessary.

N.B. The teacher should see to it that the critiques of the articles are serious both in the group study and in the hearing itself. A real effort is necessary in view of a judgment on the problem of information.

4. *Conclusion*

After the trial, the teacher should summarize or, if there is time, lead a discussion on some of these points:

—the difficulty for newspapers in fully reporting all aspects of a situation; the possible financial dependence of some papers; the elements included or excluded because of a particular political background;

—the importance of having an open and realistic spirit so as to be critical of what is read; the need for a well-formed conscience; the obligation to meet with others to discuss news events, to exchange and dialogue, to know where to look for information.

4. AUDIO-VISUAL TECHNIQUES AND AIDS

At this point, many teachers might well ask why there has been no full treatment of the use of audio-visual aids, so much a part of contemporary teaching. While there have been some references in certain chapters, it has hardly been sufficient. However, in view of the vast scope of this area, we are now preparing a separate work on this field, covering the use of photographs, movies, records, illustrations, and so forth.

APPENDIX

HOW TO BUILD A CATECHETICAL LIBRARY

MANY teachers today are looking for a convenient and simple method of organizing and classifying their catechetical materials. Careful organization and classification saves time, a definite advantage, but it also offers an area for fruitful teacher exchange and provides a concrete example of team effort.

In any school or CCD program, all of the teachers should work with the chairman in building a catechetical library. One teacher has just read an article in a magazine, another has taken a picture from a newspaper which would be useful for a discussion on community. If these can be saved and shared, each member of the teaching staff is served. Just as important, this common effort can foster unity of thought and work and spirit.

Each chairman should see to it that this service is provided for his teachers. It involves money and time, but a group of teachers is more united in the work of the whole religion program when there is a way of sharing ideas and talents.

1. PERSONNEL AND MONEY

Religion departments vary in size from school to school. Some have two or three members in the high school, others may involve fifteen or twenty. Confraternity programs frequently involve more teachers since each teacher is usually responsible for only one class a week, and there can be no doubling or tripling of classes for a teacher as happens in a regular school program.

Regardless of class size, generally, one person is needed who will be free to receive and classify material. A good library is that which provides material readily and easily. The chairman of the library should be well organized and occasionally persistent in seeking out material. Frankly, many libraries never succeed because teachers have not been reminded sufficiently to hand in material, or because they have found nothing there to use. Granted, it is a human problem, but a careful choice of librarian is a way of avoiding a number of needless problems.

Money is not a major item in this area. What may be needed are folders, looseleaf binders, some reproduction of materials by stencil or any other process of reproduction. Fortunately, today copying machines are usually available in schools and parishes. A file on stencils can be invaluable and should not be neglected. After the library has been in operation for a year, perhaps some realistic budget can be worked out and included in the annual school or parish expenditure.

2. LOCATION

In a parish CCD structure where classes may meet only once a week in the parish school, some convenient arrangement must be worked out so that teachers can obtain material during the week if it is needed. If the CCD staff is a combination of laity and religious, care should be taken that the library is not placed in the convent. While convenient for the sisters, this arrangement would hardly be of help to the laity, who would not want to interrupt the convent life in order to obtain materials. Each situation demands its own solution, but in many cases the solution may involve lay access to the school building.

Even in the regular high-school structure, the location of the library is important. A separate section in the school library is a helpful possibility, or if there is a chairman's office, perhaps the library could occupy space there. Library space is frequently at a premium; but then, so should every good religious education program.

3. THE PHYSICAL ARRANGEMENT OF MATERIAL

If many people are going to use the material, then it is necessary that it be easy to use; there should be no elaborate procedure for taking out material.

From our own experience we would advise that the following arrangement be made: a cabinet be installed containing large-size folders; each folder contains material on a separate topic, and material on any one topic can be quickly located by its identification on a label placed prominently at the top of the folder. Topics are of course within each folder, there are two divisions: one for illustrations, articles, and the like; the other set aside for catechetical outlines or programs on the same topic.

Beside or near the cabinet a box should be placed which would contain index cards, one card for each teacher and marked with his or her name. Each time a teacher needs one of the folders, he simply writes down the name of the folder on his card.

In some cases, if the school library is used, a section can be set aside for the teachers' use. Perhaps the librarian would be willing to assist in classification and distribution. Much depends on his or her schedule.

4. THE CLASSIFICATION OF MATERIAL

Proposed here is a classification that represents a compromise between age classification (childhood, pre-adolescence, adolescence, etc.) and subject grouping. From experience, this has proved to be the most practical since it takes the material covered at each age level and then divides it by subject areas.

In certain cases when the subject is treated differently according to age levels (for example, the Eucharist), double folders could be used. In this case, however, all the material on the Eucharist will be found in the age grouping where sacraments are treated. Thus if sacraments are generally treated in sophomore year, the material for the Eucharist for all age levels will be included in that classification.

5. SPECIAL METHODOLOGY SECTION

The library could also be allotted supplementary space under the general title of Methodology, subdivided as follows:

(1) syllabus for regular programs
(2) special experimental programs
(3) pastoral and methodological directions
  (a) pre-adolescence
  (b) adolescence
  (c) late adolescence or young adult

(4) group methods in religious education
(5) bibliography on religious education
(6) religious psychology of adolescents
(7) also perhaps catechetical magazines could be set aside in this area, if some arrangement can be worked out with the librarian—for example, *Living Light, Lumen Vitae, Religion Teachers' Journal.*

6. THE ORDER OF FOLDERS

The order used will not necessarily be that in which teachers give the different subjects during the year. To facilitate the use of an index, we suggest a certain traditional logical order, patterned after the general outline of the four-year course. For example, the seven sacraments are arranged one after the other, although in actuality they are usually given over a period of two years within some programs of the moral and spiritual life.

7. ILLUSTRATIONS, ARTICLES, ETC.

This division of a folder can contain whatever can aid in the preparation or illustration of any topic in religious education, whether on the doctrinal or educational level.

—doctrinal points: an article from some magazine, etc;

—illustrations, photographs:

—literary or artistic material: section from novel, lyrics for a song, quotations.

In each case, the teacher should not forget the reference: name of book, magazine, date, author, and so forth.

The rather complete outline which follows this section is only one possible approach. For a Confraternity program, teachers might work out a separate program according to the text books used or special programs that have been developed. In other cases, a particular series of texts might open up another approach.

The suggested outline, however, covers a majority of the areas that might come up in any program. Also in a time of flux in terms of text books or special programs, a larger library can be of help at present and in the years to come.

One of the first things to decide upon is the scope and direction of this library. While over-ambition can be detrimental, yet restricting oneself to a particular book or approach could impoverish this resource center.

8. SUGGESTED OUTLINE FOR THE LIBRARY

1. *Pre-Adolescence: Salvation History**

Old Testament

(1) Presenting the Bible
(2) Revelation of God
(3) Genesis: creation, fall, promise
(4) Abraham, father of believers
(5) Moses: the Exodus

(*This could apply to eighth-, ninth-, or tenth-year programs depending upon syllabus and background of the students. In many cases this material is covered at ninth-year level.)

(6) The Covenant
(7) People of God
(8) David: the Kings
(9) The Prophets
(10) The other great figures of the Old Testament: Job, Jacob, Samuel, the Maccabees
(11) The psalms and the hope of the Jewish people

New Testament

(1) Presenting the New Testament
(2) Life of Jesus: general presentation
(3) The country of Jesus: history and geography
(4) Birth and hidden life of Jesus
(5) John the Baptist: Baptism of Christ
(6) Temptations in the desert
(7) Proclamation of the Kingdom: beatitudes, parables
(8) Miracles
(9) Those with Jesus: Mary, the poor, the apostles, the children
(10) Those against Jesus: the Pharisees, Sadduccees, sinners
(11) Holy Week
(12) Resurrection, Ascension

History of the Church

(1) Presenting the history of the Church
(2) The apostles: birth of the Church
(3) The martyrs; first three centuries
(4) The progress of the Church: monasticism, Middle Ages
(5) The Reformation and the saints

(6) The missionary Church
(7) The Church in America (Britain, Australia, etc.)
(8) Post-Reformation times
(9) The Church today

2. *Adolescence: Moral Life, Spiritual Development**

Feasts and Liturgical Cycle

(1) Advent, Christmas, Epiphany
(2) Lent
(3) Easter, Ascension, Feasts of our Lord
(4) Pentecost, the Holy Spirit
(5) All Saints, heaven, and the last things
(6) Sunday

Liturgical and Sacramental Life

(1) The signs of God; the sacraments in general
(2) Baptism: liturgy and meaning; catechumenate
(3) Confirmation
(4) Penance
(5) The Eucharist

(adolescence:) liturgy and meaning; introduction to the Mass
(late adolescence:) existential and cosmic bearing of the Eucharist; summit of action and of history.

(*This could apply to ninth- or tenth- or eleventh-year programs depending upon syllabus and background of students. In many cases this material is covered at tenth-year level.)

(6) Orders
(7) Matrimony
(8) Anointing of the Sick

Problems of Life

(1) Adolescence
(2) Happiness and perfection
(3) Personality and temperament
(4) Freedom and independence
(5) Media and the Christian
(6) Community
(7) Sin
(8) Conscience
(9) Love and Friendship
(10) Purity
(11) Work
(12) Obedience and Authority
(13) Truth
(14) Poverty and Wealth
(15) Human Culture
(16) Leisure

Spiritual Life

(1) Life with Jesus Christ
(2) Prayer
(3) Vocation
(4) Penance
(5) Apostolic Mission

3. *Late Adolescence-Young Adult**

Jesus Christ and Man

(1) Creation and the human condition
(2) Ways of religious knowing
(3) Incarnation
(4) Personality and Christ's Message
(5) Redemption
(6) Easter
(7) Faith in Christ
(8) Freedom and the Holy Spirit
(9) Christ and human love
(10) Woman

The Church and the World

(1) The Church in the world today
(2) The heavenly Church
(3) Mystery of the Church
(4) Institutional Church
(5) Signs of the Church
(6) Communities outside the Church
(7) Ecumenism
(8) The missionary Church
(9) The parish
(10) Vocations

(*This could apply to tenth-, eleventh-, and twelfth-year programs depending upon syllabus and background of students. In many cases this material is covered through eleventh- and twelfth-year levels.)

(11) Councils
(12) The Church and politics

4. *Young Adult**

God

(1) Revelation
(2) Creation
(3) Atheism and faith
(4) Evolution of faith
(5) Crisis of faith
(6) Great religious developments of man: Islam, Buddhism, etc.

Eschatology

(1) Four last things
(2) Meaning of time

(*This could apply to twelfth-year and after depending upon the syllabus and programs worked out according to the background of student. In general this material is covered at twelfth-year level and above.)